MW00929564

# Race Fans:
# My Genesis and
# Evolution as a
# Triathlete

NANCY—
THANK YOU FOR YOUR SUPPORT.
ENJOY THE JOURNEY.

~ Sam Wilkinson — 2005

# Race Fans: My Genesis and Evolution as a Triathlete

*Samuel F. Wilkinson*
*Foreword by Andrew C. Lillie*

iUniverse, Inc.
New York Lincoln Shanghai

# Race Fans: My Genesis and Evolution as a Triathlete

Copyright © 2005 by Samuel F. Wilkinson

All rights reserved. No part of this book may be used or reproduced by any means, graphic, electronic, or mechanical, including photocopying, recording, taping or by any information storage retrieval system without the written permission of the publisher except in the case of brief quotations embodied in critical articles and reviews.

iUniverse books may be ordered through booksellers or by contacting:

iUniverse
2021 Pine Lake Road, Suite 100
Lincoln, NE 68512
www.iuniverse.com
1-800-Authors (1-800-288-4677)

ISBN-13: 978-0-595-37703-9 (pbk)
ISBN-13: 978-0-595-82085-6 (ebk)
ISBN-10: 0-595-37703-3 (pbk)
ISBN-10: 0-595-82085-9 (ebk)

Printed in the United States of America

*God: Thank you for endless blessings.*
*Maggie: Without your loving support none of this would be possible.*
*Alex, Claudia, and Payton: Thank you for dealing with my addiction.*
*My Parents - Tom & Portia Wilkinson: Thank you for always encouraging me.*
*Joe, Tim, Jen, Ang, Andrew & Families: You know it all started here.*
*Joe, thank you, for advocating this pursuit.*
*My Grandparents*
*My Aunts and Uncles*
*My Cousins: You are amazing people.*
*Dan & Betty Haraburda (Thanks for sharing Bassett Lake) and Britt Haraburda*
*& Olivia Reeder*
*MY FRIENDS!*
*A special thanks to Lil for his words in this literary adventure.*
*Dai, thank you for planting the seed.*
*Coaches John Soderman and Greg Meyer: Thank you for all you have done.*
*My Cross Country Teammates from Caledonia H.S., Grand Rapids C.C., and*
*Grand Valley State University*
*And*
*Baily: Thank you, my canine companion, for faithfully going with me*
*on many-o-runs.*
*You have all inspired me.*

10% of the Proceeds from this book will benefit the
*Challenged Athletes Foundation*

# Contents

# Foreword

## Andrew C. Lillie

Sam is a tall, thin man who wears a smile with his biking shorts. When he's not burning calories like some people burn valuable free time sitting on the couch watching the Shopping Network, he teaches 8-year-olds how to read, add, and behave. He has three children of his own who adore him. And a wife that not only loves him, but actually likes him.

Sam will go out of his way to help an old lady cross the street. (I'm willing to bet he'd even help a young man cross the street. But maybe that's just me.) He'll even avoid hitting old ladies who unwisely cross the street in front of him as he's burning downhill at the end of a 30-mile tempo ride, slung over his aero bars, face gripped in his aero-shades like a frightening and awe-inspiring vision from a blockbuster sci-fi movie…And he'll say hello as he blows her wig off. But don't let any of that sugar fool you. Because, if you're racing against him, he will out-compete you. I'm not saying that he'll beat you. That's the least of his concerns. But he will care more than you do. Prepare more than you do. And invest physically, mentally, and emotionally more than you do.

While you might just beat him today because your stars are in order, you better not climb up on that high horse of yours. Because…eventually…Sam will come galloping up when you least expect it and drag your sorry butt down. How do I know all this? Because Sam's dragged my sorry butt down on more than one occasion.

Luckily we remain close friends. Why? Maybe because of our commitment to good communication. Maybe because we accept each other fully. Perhaps our mutual passion for intellectual development, or our deeply held belief in the virtues of peanut-butter-and-jelly sandwiches and root-beer floats.

Our bond is also strong not in small part due to our shared joy in sport, I'm sure. We played tennis for years: many, many sets; many, many hours. I can count the times I beat Sam in a set on one hand. In fact, on two fingers. We played hoops a lot, too. Usually behind the barn or at the old elementary school with the cracked pavement. We'd bang out the old-school jams on the ghetto-blaster, pretending we were taller, stronger...blacker. And Sam would sink three-pointers one after another. I'd scramble all over the court and jump like crazy to block him. Yet like a man watching the rain fall and unable to do a darn thing about it, I spent most of my time looking up. We chased each other and our friends in wild games of woodland and swampland capture-the-flag. I'd sit still...patient, cunning...for what seemed like hours in the humid Hades of Michigan summer...in dense thickets, no less...waiting for Sam to unknowingly fall to my capture. Then he'd outrun me. Or out-cun me. At least I got better grades in science than he did.

The foregoing aside, there are two reasons I know Sam so well. We ran cross-country together. And we were best friends.

Cross-country guys are the coolest guys on the planet. At least the Caledonia, Michigan cross guys with whom I ran from 1986 to 1989. (Most of them, that is.) Why? Because we didn't show off. We didn't pretend to be better, badder, or crazier than we were. (We were already good, bad, and crazy enough.) With a few notable exceptions, we didn't admire our muscles all the time, or hope girls would dig our little, yellow nylon shorts (again, I'm now thinking of exceptions, but that's another story all together), or otherwise act like rock stars (with...one exception).

Cross-country guys are cool because we did our own thing. Every guy did his own thing with the support...or least relatively good-natured ridicule...of the other guys. We all ran pretty fast on our own. But we ran faster, and smarter, as members of the team. Especially as part of our team, with Coach Soderman at the helm. Cross-country guys are cool because they tend to be smart, and think for themselves. Those guys helped me open my mind, broaden my horizons, and become a respectable man.

Sam was the most responsible for my enlightenment because he and I share a personality trait: We talk and think and sometimes over-think our way through life. We digest, check all the angles, thrive on feedback, and need to express what's in us. And we hope to get to a better place for it all. (Of course, sometimes we just spin our wheels, like back in the day when we'd analyze the girls in our lives for hours on end, leaving little weekend time to *actually spend time* with any of them. Luckily we're both happily married now. I like to think our studies paid off in dividends.)

As Sam has said to me many times, I say to him: Sam: "You're a gentleman and a scholar." The "scholar" part is why you have numerous pages of first-person multi-sport narrative to read when you finish with me. Sam loves to tell his story. Always has. It's one of the things I like most about him because he entertains me and I know he'll listen to my stories. He loves life, knows it's worth living to the best of his ability, and likes to share his journey with those folks he cares about. You, reader, are luckily on that list.

Sam also enjoys writing. If you're one of the Race Fans who has opened her Inbox to an installment from the frontiers of Wilkinson multi-sport land many times over the last few years, you already know this. If you're new to this, you're lucky. Because this isn't one of those personal essay collections that sucks, that makes you want to vomit in the road. No, this one is actually *worth reading*. Because Sam cares about the readers. He tries to give you what he would want, an exciting story about a man's struggles with his ambitions, his body, his spirit, his mind. You'll find yourself riding next to Sam as he plans to overtake his next target. You'll be with him as he sets out his gear at the transition. You'll share his pain and bask a little in his glory. (You *won't*, however, shower with him after he gets home. This isn't one of *those* books of personal essays).

The "gentleman" part is why Sam put this thing together. As he's giving you a peek into his passion, he's trying to inspire you to put down this book, pull on some shorts and a smile, and try it for yourself. I'm betting you will.

# Preface

As many of you know, over the years I have been sending out e-mail reports of my events. Some of these accounts have been misplaced, but the ones I have are included in this compilation. I started printing them in 2000, so some of you by some strange twist of fate may have some earlier "lost" episodes of "Race Fans" not in hardcopy. You will also notice that not all of the events are triathlons, but all of the events are in some way related to my experience as a triathlete.

Through sharing my *Race Fans* accounts, I have been encouraged by several people I trust to publish my accounts, and share them with others. What you are reading now is a product of many years of documented experiences. I only intended to compile my accounts in order to share them with my children when they are grown. Basically I'm just a triathlete who teaches third grade; what do *I* know about writing a book for crying out loud? Anyway, I have now opened this up to you and I am confident you will enjoy the journey.

# Introduction:
# My Genesis and Evolution

It is difficult to say where my triathlon beginnings are because I'm not entirely certain what I should qualify as training and competing in multi-sport. When I was quite young, I don't believe I ever walked to or from my neighbors whom I frequently visited. I either ran or rode my bike. Was I training then for what would later be formal participation in multi-sport? Some might say it doesn't count until one consciously puts one foot in front of the other in an effort to better ones ability in competition. Well if this is the case, I guess I began in the spring of 1985 while preparing for my eighth grade track season. Regardless, running to the neighbors and asking if they wanted to ride bikes to go swimming in the river, may not count as efforts toward bettering my abilities, but it sure set the groundwork for the love of multi-sport I have today.

If my childhood was my foundation, then cross country, road racing, inspirational family, friends, and coaches created the springboard which molded me into the triathlete I have become. Self-discipline, determination, and dedication can only go so far without the support of others, and support has never been lacking for me. This assistance is what has inspired me to share in writing my journey in multi-sport over the past decade.

## Cross Country

I was privileged to have great coaches while running cross-country in high school, at Caledonia, and at Grand Rapids Junior College. Coach John Soderman, who will forever be known as "Coach" was the winning-est coach in football, wrestling, track, and cross-country, at Caledonia High School. He had yet to dabble in golf as a coach, but if he had the result would likely have been the same. Having Greg Meyer, who might possibly be forever known as "The last American to win the *Boston Marathon*" as my coach was an exceptional experience during my time at Grand Rapids Junior College (GRJC). I only had the good fortune of being coached by him for one year, but he extended me more than I thought was possible.

"Gentlemen," Coach Soderman would say while addressing us in his booming, authoritative voice, "How's everyone feeling today?" Coach always cared about how we were feeling, but was prepared to have us feeling differently by the end of practice. Coach was the kind of guy you knew cared a lot about you, and his athletes wanted to work their butts off for him out of respect, if nothing else. He had a calming way about him, even in the heat of a major event. During a *High School Class B, Regional Cross-Country Finals* where we produced a championship effort, I recall him shouting out, "Sam, you need to get some guys in blue!" Of course I had an idea for what he meant because he briefed us on the teams to beat. However, I didn't pay too much attention to which teams to beat, because I was out there to give everything I had no matter what. Coach's voice did not carry a sense of urgency or panic, he simply stated the facts. Ok, fair enough, get the guys in blue. I also remember looking up to the pack in front of me and seeing three different shades of blue, and this on as many different jerseys. Not knowing which blue he wanted, I just went after all of them. When someone said "Coach" in Caledonia, there was little question, unless you were new to town, to whom you were referring.

Having both been products of the Coach Soderman Cross Country Machine, my friend and teammate Tim Hodgkinson, and I called Coach Meyer "Coach," but referred to him in conversations as Greg. This is not to say we did not respect Coach Meyer, because we certainly did, it just that "Coach" was somebody else. "Alright, you are going to go around that tree," Coach Meyer instructed, as he was pointing out our 400 meter loop at Richmond Park, "down along that tree line, turn at the last tree," still guiding us with his finger, "and over to that tree, and back." The directions appear ambiguous, but it was obvious to us while he pointed out our course. "Ok, you're going to do four times, one mile repeats in 4:50." We all must have expressed shock in our own ways, because he then said, "What...too fast?" I didn't answer; I just kept my eyes on the ground while searching my brain for any time I had run close to that. I came up empty, but was geared up to try to make today the day. "Ok," I thought, "if he thinks I can do it, maybe I can. Let's do this!" Finally my good friend Mark (Roach) said, "Yeah, that's a bit quick." His comments opened a flood of nods and "Uh-huhs." Mark was also quick to say what we were all thinking though, when he quickly came back with, "But we'll do the best we can if that's what you want us to do." Coach Meyer altered the time 5:15's and we hit the mark, but it took everything we had to do it.

Coach Meyer prompted me to reassess my predetermined abilities and had me performing beyond what I thought was possible. His high expectations caused me to raise my own bar, and whether or not I always met the challenge, I always ended up surprising myself. He inspired me, and through my efforts, I inspired myself with his tutelage.

While Coach Soderman instilled self-discipline, teamwork, and tactical thinking, Coach Meyer forged a spirit which challenged my self-determined position as a runner.

Not mentioning my cross-country teammates from Caledonia High School (CHS), Grand Rapids Junior College (GRJC), and then Grand Valley State University (GVSU) who were essential in the development of my current athletic self, would be dishonorable. My greatest bonds with my friends have been fashioned in one way or another through running and training. Andy Lillie, Dai Wessman, and Tim Hodgkinson, who were some of my best friends, were all from our CHS cross-country team. Though our contact has become less frequent, our bond remains strong. There are many deserving to be mentioned, but I can't list them all, so the following are just a few: I had the pleasure of running with Bryan Harrison at CHS, who I ran around with many times in my childhood in our rural neighborhood. My wife's cousin Lin is married to Mike Nickles, a friend of mine who was a CHS harrier in a class of strong runners. Furthermore, there are such great influences from CHS as Dave Smith, Mark and Todd Cherpes, Mark Prins, and of course Jeff Groendyke, who would have taken my varsity spot my junior year if it hadn't been for a back injury.

At GRJC, not only was I introduced to a great motivator and inspiration, and now longtime friend Mark Roach, but also to several other runners who helped make me a better runner. In addition, GVSU offered such influences as Josh Reynolds, and Pete Bodary, who are still good friends of mine. Additional teammates who have influenced me include Sean Donovan, Roger Bloomer, and Ryan Knapp. Many, many miles have been logged with my teammates, my friends…my *brotha's-from-otha'-motha's*. Regardless of conditions and perceived misery at times, I can't think of one of those runs I would take back. Great memories stay with me, and I thank each and every one of my teammates for being a part of my life. I take one or several of these guys with me in my heart and mind on some of my runs even today. The inspiration they have given me still lives.

## Dai Wessman: Planting the Seeds of Triathlon

I stood there on the beach with my heart pounding, as the horn blew, and the athletes entered the cool waters, marking the start of the *Seahorse Triathlon*; the first triathlon I had ever witnessed in person. My good friend Dai asked if I would like to go along with him to a triathlon he was doing and be his support crew. My actual "job" amounted to helping him carry his gear from his car prior to the start, and carting it back after the conclusion of the event. Little did I know, this would be one of my first steps toward becoming a triathlete.

What a thrill for me to see my friend in action. People clad in black neoprene were emerging from the water after covering two loops totaling two kilometers of swimming, which seemed to me longer than anyone should be asked to swim *before* cycling and running! Dai broke the water and made his way up the sandy trail which led the athletes to the transition area. I ran like a rabbit through the woods standing before me, in order to see Dai perform his transition. "Way to go Dai!" I shouted, totally pumped. Paying attention to every detail, as he has always been known to do, he very quickly-but-carefully transformed from swimmer to cyclist. He trotted his bike to the mounting area, hopped on his bike, and tore off down the road. "Keep it up Dai!" I yelled, "Way to go!" There was an endless stream of people heading out in pursuit of the leaders or their own personal goals. These triathletes giving it their all came in all shapes, sizes, ages, and abilities

While Dai pedaled his way over the 40k course, I waited. After what seemed like hardly any time at all, he was back. "Way to go Dai!" There was no need to get creative with my encouraging words, because he didn't have time to listen anyway. Like most athletes, I'm sure he was just glad I was there giving him some love. With his helmet off and with his running shoes slipped on, he was in hunt of those who came before him. "Go Dai! Go get 'em!" I ranted as he disappeared around the corner.

Again, in what seemed like short order, there was Dai trudging up the last hill, and it was a mother-of-a-hill. I positioned myself halfway up nature's obstacle to verbally kick him in the rear, as he worked the last bit of the event's real estate. "You can do it Dai! Dig deep! Way to go! Go! Good job! Go!"…and he went.

I don't remember how well Dai placed, or what his time was that day, but I remember thinking how awesome he was. In my eyes, he was a man among men, and he deserved every stitch required to assemble the *Seahorse Triathlon* commemorative race t-shirt and any other accolades he received that day. I remember thinking how cool the whole experience was and how I was inspired as I traveled back from his Allegan home, to continue to train hard and become an ass kickin' road racin' machine. What I didn't realize that day, but now know, was how significant that day was in my development in becoming a triathlete.

After I became a fairly established triathlete myself, Dai again planted a seed, but this time for racing the half-Ironman distance. In the summer of 1997, Dai informed me he would be doing the *Muncie Endurathon ½ Ironman*, in Muncie, Indiana. This was a stop for him on his way home from Ohio State University where he was in the process of earning his Masters Degree in Exercise Physiology. Maggie and I decided to drive down from Michigan and provide moral support, and escort him home after the event. At this point I had done several triathlons, but it was early in my career, and doing a ½ Ironman seemed like quite a daunt-ing task. Swimming 1.2 miles, followed by cycling 56 miles, and then tag on run-ning 13.1 miles…*shazam* man! I knew I could run 13.1 miles, and thought I could probably swim 1.2 miles with more training, and perhaps cycle 56 miles if I built up to it, but for me to do this, it would have to be completed on different days, *not* one right after the other! Not only did Dai complete all three consecu-tively, he smashed all three, and completed the event well under five hours. This mind you, is a time highly sought after for this distance, but it's not easily obtain-able. Yet again, I left awed and inspired, and now thinking, "Maybe *some day* I will be able to do one of these things." The seed had settled in the fertile soil of my growing passion for triathlon.

Not only has Dai motivated me and challenged me, but he has supported me in many ways. He has been quick to provide me with advice on many matters I have sought out. He has encouraged me, trained with me, and raced with me (mostly in front of me). Purchasing my Litespeed was even inspired by Dai's ownership and fondness of his own. Racing on carbon fiber, HED, H3, three-spoked wheels would not be possible without his generous donation. I believe I am most impacted however by his leadership, by way of his example. Thank you, Dr. Dylan E. Wessman. You are the man!

# Road Race Love Affair

My first road race took place the summer of 1989, at the *Plainwell Classic*, in Plainwell, Michigan. I wanted to see what kind of shape I was in, because I decided to try out for the Grand Rapids Junior College Cross-Country team in the fall. This race ignited quite a spark, because I was hooked. I ran at least six road races a year while I was still in college, and after I graduated with my first undergrad degree, I raced over thirteen races a year, for two years. I raced any-where from 5k to the marathon.

I spent a long time chasing down 5ks and 10ks before I got the long distance bug. Breaking sixteen minutes in the 5k became an obsession of mine after my college cross-country career came to an end, and though I had many great work-outs, and several excellent races attempting this feat, it simply never materialized. The closest I got was 16:14 at the *Tricks-or-Treats 5k* in Dutton, Michigan. Fifteen seconds. You wouldn't think five seconds per mile would be such a daunt-ing gap to bridge, but there it was. I still believed there was untapped potential in me that required awakening, but it was not to be found in five kilometers.

Another avenue was taken as I ran 20ks, 25ks, half-marathons, 10-milers, and marathons. I loved road racing, and I couldn't get enough of it…and then I got injured.

## From Injury to Inspiration

The summer of 1995 welcomed an unwanted visitor by way of my Achilles tendon injury realizing its full potential. Its onset was likely in the fall of 1994. I was determined to figure this injury out, fix it, and be done with it. Unfortunately, healing and getting back on track was a very long process, which led me feeling helpless, frustrated, and dejected. I ultimately resorted to pool running and stationary bike workouts, which was really the beginning of something I had yet to consider, as the seeds that had settled in the soil years before began to take root. After pool running started to get really old, I decided to dabble in lap swimming. At first I would swim mini-laps in the deep end, away from the "real" lap swimmers, in the actual swim lanes. As my swimming became more proficient, I gained enough courage to swim with the sharks, so-to-speak, and I moved to the swim lanes. You know the ones with black lines on the bottom and the blue and white lane markers? It turned out to be a good decision, and I was not as bad as I thought. I read a lot about technique, and asked questions of anyone I knew who swam. I finally became a swimmer, and I donned a Speedo and pool sandals with a twisted sense of entitlement.

My Achilles tendon was getting stronger, the cycling I began on a stationary bike and my mountain bike became more frequent and extended, and my swimming was taking shape. I began looking longingly through the *Gazelle Sports Race Calendar* to see what races I probably couldn't run, and I saw the *Mark Mellon Triathlon* noted. The main event was a 1k/50k/10k, but that is not what caught my eye. It was the short course being offered that captured my imagination. The short course triathlon was 200yd/10mi/2mi. I put one, and one, and one together while considering my latest athletic endeavors, and came up with *triathlon*! Little did I know, this would be the event that would launch me into my life as a triathlete. After this experience, I could hardly contain myself thinking of the events I would attempt in the seasons to come. The seed that had taken root now sprouted with vigor to the surface.

## Experiencing and Sharing the Love

I have not yet decided whether to be proud, or ashamed, that the sport of triathlon has seduced me, and has become a compulsion, which I am dedicated and addicted to. Through the progression of time, and the experiences I have had, triathlon has become a driving force in my life. I will not say God and family are beneath triathlon, because certainly they are not. In fact both allow it, support it, and encourage it. Admittedly however, triathlon truly moves me physically, emotionally, and spiritually in ways I can't fully explain. From the seed planted by Dai's model, and the sprout of my newfound enjoyment of all three sports, triathlon evolved in my life and has become a mighty oak.

I have done triathlons of various distances from sprint to the half-Ironman, and have proven to myself that I can be competitive in duathlon as well. Rounding out my seasons in the top third in the nation, region, and *Michigan Grand Prix Triathlon Series,* for my age-group has been the norm. In 2003, I won the *Michigan Grand Prix Series Duathlon Series* for my age group, and was named *All-Regional* (Michigan, Indiana, Illinois, and Kentucky is the Mid-East Region for the *United States Triathlon Association,* to which I am a member).

I am proud of the accomplishments I have earned and I will continue to strive to achieve more, but the accolades are not where most of my joy is found, but rather in the experiences I have gained. For example: In the summer cycling at predawn, on Sunday mornings when the sun is still contemplating showing itself, I pedal silently alone down the road, only hearing the sound of my tires wheeling down the pavement. I am moving along knowing my ride has just begun, while so many are sleeping and I'm overcome with peace. The profound nostalgia I experience while running into town and around "*Small Block*" where I ran so many times with my Caledonia cross-country teammates can be surreal. My footfalls on the gravel segment of the run, put me in a trance, and take me back to a simpler time. Swimming around Bassett Lake with confidence and my body gliding horizontally forward is as close as I can get to flying under my own power. Finally, putting it all together and sharing it with friends and family on race day is the culmination of my satisfying efforts, experiences, and my joy, in the sport I love.

# Family

Participating in triathlon started out pretty innocently and did not consume a great deal of family time, but when I started, I was doing all short course triathlons, and there was just Maggie and I to share the time. My addiction has grown, and my sights have been focused on longer events, and events requiring greater travel. Time has passed and our family has grown. Now there is Alex, Claudia, and Payton included in the mix. Amen. Training time is something which requires careful planning around naps and other obligations. Racing is another creature which involves getting up very early, getting children dressed, and getting out the door with baby joggers, sippy-cups, blankets, and fruit snacks. Finding time to train and race is complicated now and again, but Maggie and our children are always supportive. I love them and thank them very much. I am glad I can share my love for the sport with them, and am grateful I have not been kicked out of the house for my overindulgence. Fortunately for me, they support my passion. My heart still melts when it is pounding in my chest, and I'm giving it my all in a race and I hear the words, "Go Daddy go! Go Daddy go!" For me…it doesn't get any better than this.

# Maggie

Maggie has been and continues to be my biggest sponsor and fan since the beginning of my multi-sport adventures. She is always willing to listen to me talk about training rides, runs, swims, and every detail, about every race, I have ever done. She has gone through the highs and lows, and has always been encouraging. The *Race Fans* reports from my events are nothing compared to the earfuls Maggie deals with. The questions she deals with…*oh* the questions. The fact that she has not thrown a brick at me amazes me still. "What did you think of my transition today?" I would ask, "Do you think if I put my glasses on first, and then my helmet, I could get out sooner?" It isn't that I expect her to know the answers to these things, but she allows me to use her as my sounding board. "What do you think, should I focus on triathlons or duathlons this season? I mean, I think I could really contend in duathlon, but I am just so drawn to triathlon." Although, I look equally absurd in the eyes of everyday citizens, I'm sure she loves this question: "Do you think I should wear my tri-briefs or my tri-shorts for this race?" She is kind enough *not* to say, "Sam, you look like a skinny fool no matter what you choose, so roll the dice and be done with it already."

She has been patient with my expenditures as well. From buying expensive bike parts and service every year, to training apparel, sports bars, paying heavy race fees, generating travel expenses, and so forth she *still* loves me. She cares for our children while I train and race. I have been doing triathlon since 1995, and she has been in attendance for all but four events, and I have done about seven or eight a year. I missed her dearly each time she wasn't there.

I bought *another* bike this year. I think I'm losing my mind and being a selfish fat cat, even though I know the benefits of such a purchase, but she says, "Sam, I think you should." She is my biggest fan, and I am hers.

## Team Dust For Breakfast

One of my favorite events of all time involved a lot of travel, serious commitment, and pain in the butt (mostly my brother Joe's and Tim's butts, truth be told). At the conception of the idea for my brothers and me to compete in an adventure race together, Tim and Joe were living in Mississippi, and Andrew and I were living in Michigan. I figured Tim and Joe could drive up to Southern Ohio, and Andrew and I could drive down. It would be about five hours for

Andrew and I, while Tim and Joe would travel more like ten. Well after we committed to the race, I registered us and booked a hotel. From the time I registered us, to the time of the event, Tim transferred to Yellowstone National Park, in Montana, and Joe and Andrew moved to California. Despite the severe geographical conundrum, we all showed up and toed the line together. I love these guys! Andrew and I did end up driving down together after Andrew flew in from the west coast, and Tim and Joe drove over to meet us, but their drive turned out to be more of an adventure than the race itself. It was exhilarating for me to compete with my brothers. I was in seventh heaven throughout the entire event. Not only did I have the opportunity to do what I love, I got to do it side-by-side with my brothers! How cool is that! The account of the race is in *Race Fans 2003*. Take a look.

## Triathlon Family Members

When I first got into the sport of triathlon, I didn't recognize anyone at the races, but after a while I began to recognize many. Triathletes in this area are not far removed from a traveling circus, insomuch that, in the summer months we move from one town to the next putting on our show, in our silly costumes. Ann Arbor, Niles, and Gaylord are just a few of the tour stops. The veterans of the *Michigan Grand Prix Series* recognize, and compete against each other at varied venues. We either, show up the day before an event and pitch our tents, or we set out very early in the morning to arrive in time to push ourselves to our limits. Here's a short list of some the triathlon icons in our area. The Hoag family, whom we attempt to get a camping spot next to each year in Gaylord, has been a connection we probably have had the longest, and their connections with others has brought us closer to our area's triathlon family. Ricky Green is a regular who races everything, all the time and is a rock. Tom and Corrine Strumberger are a talented couple, who smoke me on Tuesdays and Thursdays in the Middleville pool, and are only beginning to realize their potential. Another important notable is Kevin Miller who is a gifted runner and an amazing triathlete. Adriano Rosa is another who is a force to be reckoned with and is a fine craftsman of custom orthodics. Scott Miller is not only an avid triathlete, but is a physical therapist that has helped put me together again, on more than one occasion. The list goes on, and while the family grows, there's still room for those who are inspired.

# My Initiation...

## Mark Mellon Short Course Triathlon, August 1995
## (200yd/10mi/2mi)

We stayed at the Grand Hotel in Gaylord, the night before the race, and there was a thunderstorm when the morning was still dark. When the alarm sounded, the rain still came down, and I remember saying something like, "It better stop raining. I mean, we came all this way and paid the race fee, and I *want* to do this thing." The rain mercifully ceased and we drove only a few miles to what would be my first triathlon.

As we entered Otsego Lake County Park, I was pretty well stressed. Where do I park? Where do I put my bike? Should I really be wearing this excessively gross deep-purple, Speedo-type suit that I fetched at Meijer, which I found alone on a sale rack, and with its final mark down? I settled down after we parked. I found the short course rack, positioned my gear, and got my bearings. Stress turned to full throttled excitement. "This is *so* cool," I thought. "I'm here. I'm doing this!" Maggie took my picture under the banner reading, *Coors Light, Start, Mark Mellon Memorial Triathlon.* I had arrived.

*The Swim*: I positioned myself in the back, away from the "real triathletes," because I didn't want to get in their way. They could have their race; I just wanted to enjoy myself and finish. Once the race started I ran in the water until it was up to my shoulders instead of attempting to swim right away. I was freaked out about swimming in the crowd, and running in the crowd wasn't so bad. There were probably only fifty or less in the whole race, but it seemed like a lot more at the time. I started swimming, but it was nothing like swimming in the pool at GRCC on my lunch hours. My head was up, I was looking all around, and I could not find a rhythm or the courage to put my head down to swim normally. A lot of energy was being expended, but nevertheless I was passing people. After rounding the first buoy, the pack as it was, thinned out and I finally brought myself to put my head down, and swim like I had practiced. This did not last long however, because as soon as I could touch, and that was only a minute later, I started running again. So, I probably actually "swam" about 50 of the 200 yards. I was grateful to reach the shore.

*T1*: From the waterfront we ran upon many floor mats placed on the ground to protect our feet, and the transition wasn't far. When I reached my bike, I was taking my sweet time. I dried myself from head to toe with my towel, put on my socks, shoes, and other items for the ride, and wheeled my mountain bike out of transition. I stopped and smiled at Maggie so she could take my picture. She snapped a quick photo then shouted, "Get going! You're in 10th place!" Instantly my triathlon experience turned from event to race.

*The Bike*: I tore off on my heavy, wide-bodied bike, in pursuit of excellence. I was huffing and puffing realizing I was out too fast. My heart rate was soaring, but my will was strong. My peddling was powered by serious ambition and trepidation. I really had no idea what effect cycling this hard followed by running would have on me. I didn't know if I would be able to get off my bike, and then run like the wind, or if I would get off the bike and crumble into the dirt. The turn-around point came and I saw I was now in sixth place. I was on a mission to get back without anyone passing me. At times I would dangerously rest my forearms on my handlebars to try to gain the advantage of those who had aero bars. Mostly though, I just churned my legs as fast and furiously as I could until I reached the park again.

I racked my bike by putting the kickstand down, put my racing flats on, and the footrace began.

*The Run*: I held my sixth place position on the bike, and hoped to make an impact on the run. I remember feeling my bike-to-run legs for the first time. My legs were heavy like they normally felt at the *end* of a footrace. I pushed the pace hoping I would be able to run swiftly in the state I was in, and discovered the heavy-leg feeling does go away. As I headed toward the first aid station, after having acknowledged four runners ahead of me, I wasn't sure where they turned around. I shouted, "Is this the turn around?" The response from the volunteers was troubling, "I don't know." My next question was easy, "Did the other guys turn around here?" The answer that followed was even more stressful, "I'm not sure." I looked at my watch and determined that I had gone at least a mile and decided it was the turn-around. I got to the table and took a paper cup of water, put some of it down, and discarded it, all in the same motion. Heading back I was looking to catch the guy I could see in the not-so-far-off distance. I tracked him down, but I was unable to make any ground on those in front of me. I came barreling down the last downhill stretch of Otsego County Park like I was going to win, and when I finished I felt as though I had.

What a rush! I talked Maggie's ear off about the race all the way home. Since she had been at many of my road (foot) races, this chatter was not new, but this time it was different. On this day, I was officially initiated into triathlon.

# The '90s: Pre Race Fans

There is a big gap in the *Race Fans* accounts because I didn't begin composing them regularly until 2000, so this section is to fill in the blanks a little. What follows are some highlights from these years.

## 1996

My first full season of triathlon was in 1996, and the highlight of this season was the absolute thrill I felt every single time I towed the line of an event. I was ambitious, and this provided me with many learning opportunities along the way. However, the most remarkable event of this season was my first *Reeds Lake Triathlon.* Dai was up from Ohio State University visiting his parents in Allegan, and his first weekend back he competed in the *Niles Triathlon* (.5mi/17.5mi/5mi), and he was slated to join me to compete in the *Reeds Lake Triathlon* the following weekend. Understand that Dai had been doing triathlons for some time at this point, and he was certainly my superior in the sport I virtually just discovered the previous summer.

Relative to cycling, swimming and running were my stronger areas at this point, and I provided an effort early that was surprising to my guest. Shortly after he exited the water, Dai heard a familiar voice close behind him saying, "Good job". A voice, I might add, he did not anticipate hearing. Expecting to come in and show me what's what in the sport of triathlon, Dai suddenly realized he was in for more than he had bargained for. Somewhere in the shuffle of the transition I lost track of him, and I didn't see him again until the turn-around on the bike. He had already made the hairpin turn and was a good quarter mile ahead of me when I was still approaching the cones marking the turn. We shouted encouragement to each other, and moved on. At this point, his much more powerful cycling strength left me behind. I didn't see him again until during the run.

After T2 I had a good jump on the run and was feeling strong and fast. I remember being surprised when I looked up and saw Dai around mile two. We ran together for a short time before I pulled away. I expected him to come along at any time in the remaining miles, but it didn't happen. I looked over my shoulder as I rounded the last turn, but didn't see him. I knew that wasn't enough information because there was a hill that obstructed my view, and I clearly understood that he could be crankin' up the pace, and there was still about 600 meters or so left. I accelerated out of fear and excitement, and though I was going on fumes, I didn't want to risk anything. I went to the next gear and motored down the descent to the finish line at a pace faster than I thought I had in me. Dai came in not too far behind me. Being the gentlemen he is we exchanged compliments on a race well done…but he was *not* done. There would be another day.

## 1997

Finishing the *Resolution Run* (4 mile) in 24:53 and then completing the *Old Kent River Band Run* (25K) in 1:41:57 compelled me to feel optimistic about what the 1997 triathlon season would bring, and it didn't disappoint. However, the epic battle of the season took place in Columbus, Ohio. Dai invited me down to his home turf to break out the goggles, wheels, and racing flats, to see what could be done about his disappointing performance the previous year at Reeds Lake.

The *Wendy's International Triathlon* had an exceptional venue. The point-to-point swim was very cool. I remember treading water with Dai while we awaited the start of our wave. This would almost be the final time I would see him throughout the entire event.

The horn blew and we made our way amongst the crowd of equal-age-groupers, and we could see the shore about 50 meters away with spectators cheering for us and walking along the beach. I saw in front of me a person I thought was Dai, but no such luck. When I exited the water I didn't see him anywhere. Maggie, who was there lending support, gave me the news that he was a minute ahead of me.

Once on my bike, I hammered the best I could in attempts to reel him in, but still I never saw him on the single-looped course. After exchanging wheels for shoes, I continued my pursuit with high hopes and the idea that I still had a chance to catch him. I saw him in the middle of the run where there was an out-and-back section, and he was looking strong and determined. Meanwhile, I was trying to get enough oxygen and to keep my heart from bursting out of my chest, as my weary legs did their best to move me forward.

The finish found me stumbling over the line, grabbing some water, and noticing Dai casually exchanging accounts of the event with his OSU buds. Whew…I was whipped and put back in my place. Being served humble pie by Dai was not terribly disappointing for me, because I knew I got away with something the previous year at Reed's anyway. It was an incredible race and we all had an excellent time. This was the last time I would race Dai head-to-head, but I didn't stop chasing after his times at different events and distances.

## 1998

This was a strong season for me with many quality performances which I can look back at and be proud. This year also marked my first taste of duathlon in the form of the *Steelcase Duathlon* (5k/30k/5k). The event would later motivate me to give duathlon a shot, and ultimately win my age-group in duathlon (30–34), in the *Michigan Grand Prix Series,* in 2003. I remember finishing thinking it was pretty cool…but it wasn't triathlon. The special part of this event though was bringing home my first of two highly-sought-after *Steelcase Duathlon* office chairs, which were given away to the top three in every age-group.

## 1999

This is the year I discovered the *Michigan Grand Prix Series,* and I attempted to reach the highest place I could in my age-group. I had strung together some respectable efforts and landed a fourth place finish, for males aged 25–29 for the series. By the end of this season, I was thinking seriously about doing my first ½ Ironman the following year.

## 2000–2005

The advent of the *Race Fans* reports officially got going in 2000. The reader base began with a handful of family members and a few friends. It has since expanded to more family members, numerous friends, and the rumor of "for-wards" to some I later became aware of, and some I still don't know about.

After gathering all of the *Race Fans* reports, I discovered I am missing more than I expected. I believe the cause for this is that I didn't save the reports with the forethought of a book to follow. So, you will notice several events noted in my race results/times pages that do not have written accounts.

# Chapter One: Race Fans 2000

### Trail ½ Marathon, April 2000
### 13.1 Miles of Trail Running

The day started out a bit chilly (45 degrees-ish), but it was fine by me. I sported my black, mesh, well-ventilated, Nike cap (I am still Nike saturated but…I got a deal at the Nike outlet while visiting my sister Ang in MN), a sleeveless, roughly scissor-cut *Gazelle Sports* t-shirt, my black INSPORT shorts, my grey Pearl Izumi "trail" socks, and my Saucony dogs on my feet. I was ready to do battle with my demons. My game plan was to attack the hills and relax/recover, as best I could on the flats and downhills. This proved to be an effective method for about eight miles. The monstrous hills were relentless and began to take their toll. Although I continued to work the hills, the tempo I carried was not what it was in the earlier miles. I began my steady-as-she-goes pace to simply maintain, and this was wonderful until about eleven and a quarter miles. At this point the trail demons put it all on the table. I ascended a steep 100 meter grade, took the curve at the top, only to find a steeper and slightly longer hill of about 125 meters, which was followed by a gradual hill of about twenty-five more meters! I was reduced to the speed of a severely overweight man in a cotton sweat suit, wearing headphones, and jogging on a Sunday morning. I thought walking would be inevitable, but I kept repeating in my mind, "Test your resolve." It seemed to work, because I conquered the hills and went on to mile twelve with confidence. At this point, I said to myself, "I can do a mile. I can do this." My pace quickened…slightly, let's be honest. I held on to the finish where I scored a 1:35:35 (roughly 5 minutes faster than I expected, and 5 minutes slower than the first time I completed this event). I celebrated with the post-race refreshments, and sucked down water and Gatorade. Josh (Reynolds) cramped mid-way and soldiered in posting a respectable 1:47-something. The next day found my legs tired and my hips somewhat tender. Nevertheless, a good time was had by all.

## Ludington Lakestride, June 2000
## 13.1 Miles

The sun was not up yet, as it was only 4:35 a.m. We dragged ourselves out of bed and hit the open road to Ludington, Michigan. We arrived in plenty of time to get my race number, use the porta-potty, and warm-up. There was a chill in the air, with temps only in the upper 50's and a wind from the northwest. Conditions were fit for running a half-marathon in mid-June. I was hoping to run a 1:30:00 or better, maybe a 1:29-something. I started out comfortable, and ran through the first mile in 6:30-ish. I intended to run through mile one closer to 6:50, but I felt relaxed and at ease, so I told myself to just go with it. By mile four I was running on a wooded trail, which was a good mental and physical mix for me. At mile six I emerged from the woods and trotted down a sizeable sand dune, ran through the state park driveway, and out the park exit, to the road along the lakeshore. The wind was now at my back and the road was open and ready for whatever I had to throw at it. I recognized my pace was still in the area of 6:30s, and I was still feeling relaxed, so I went on unconcerned. However, upon reaching mile nine my legs started to become drained, but I had to consider I had been ascending a hill for the past three-quarters of a mile. So, I told myself to press on and be patient. The ten mile marker showed itself and I needed more of a pick-me-up than just a drink of water the kind volunteers at the aid station were offering. I happily recalled I had stashed a *GU* gel pack in my shorts pocket for such an occasion, and I began to take it bit by bit. By the eleven mile aid station, I was feeling stronger and my confidence was high. "You can do this!" I coached myself, "Give me two more miles like this!" After the twelve mile marker there is a quarter mile hill, which is not generally welcomed at this point, but today I embraced it knowing once I got over it, I would be able to pick it up another notch while heading for the homestretch. With a half mile left, I was picking up the pace. Soon I saw the starting banner, this meant I only had a quarter mile to go. "Let's do this!" I thought. My pace became faster still, and I was carrying a strong clip as I sped down the straightaway, and I crossed the finish line with a time of 1:23:38 (*four minutes faster than my previous best ½ marathon*)! Needless to say...I smiled that day.

## Clark Lake Triathlon, July 2000
## (.5mi/13mi/4mi)

As nearly all my races begin, it started dark and too damn early for even the rooster. This is not a complaint, and I am certainly not bitter, it's just the nature of the beast. The buckets of rain had not yet been poured, but a light mist informed me that today would not be filled with sunshine. Strangely…maybe not too strange for someone like me, my biggest concern was I didn't really want to ride my new, bitchin' Litespeed, titanium, triathlon bike in the rain. Under these circumstances, one swims and gets wet, one rides, but slows down on the corners, one runs and finds his/her socks soggy. The big thing is however, is that once your bike gets soaked to the core for the first time, it's just not the same.

Anyway, I set my gear up in the transition area. I carefully and methodically placed my various shoes and other items in plastic bags, hoping to keep something dry. The rain started coming down steadily and at times in sheets. My station was ready and I stood there pleased with my arrangement, but still was irritated about my beautiful bike being rained on.

*The Swim*: On this day there was little-to-no opportunity to warm-up properly, which would later lead to my swimming horror story. The start of the 2000 *Clark Lake Triathlon* was right on time…8:30 a.m. We were off! I decided I was going to have a good swim here because, for some reason, I usually don't. With this motivation, I took off like I was going to win the whole dang thing! The triathlon gods had something else in mind however. After only about 150 meters into the race, I experienced what some call "the octopus". My wetsuit began what seemed to be a major squeeze around my neck and chest. The sensation I experienced was such that I was convinced I was running out of air, was dieing, and would be sinking to the bottom of the lake, never to be seen again. Panic was beginning to set in. I told myself to relax, and that I *was* getting air. Relax…hmm; didn't work. Panic at this point was in full swing. I looked around for a life boat, a surfboard, a blow-up dinosaur for kids…It didn't matter, as long as it could save me! The next boat was miles away. Ok, seventy-five feet at best, but it seemed like a long way. I continued to propel myself forward trying not to disturb the forty-five swimmers behind me…chasing me really! I turned on my back and started kicking my feet vigorously. I was pulling on my wetsuit at the collar in efforts to get more air. Nothing. I pulled the Velcro strap off the back of my suit. Nothing. I pulled the zipper down about six inches. Ah yes…air at last!!! I managed to get some air and gained my composure. I was embarrassed, and frankly felt like an ass. I knew my fear was mostly irrational, and I was losing time to my competitors who were swimming like normal people. I was irritated that I was freaking out and dragging half the lake into my wetsuit. "Ok, relax, you can do this," I told myself. I zipped and sealed my wetsuit again, turned back over and started swimming again. I could breathe, and I kept telling myself to relax. It seemed to work because I began passing people and was not on the lake's bottom. This whole freak-out session was only thirty seconds or less, but it was enough to allow me to appreciate the ability to breathe air. Ultimately, I did finish the swim in (guess how many seconds slower than last year?) thirty seconds slower than last year.

*The transition* (T1) was about 100 meters away, so I jogged, appreciating the fact that I couldn't drown at this point…though it was raining rather heavily. Reaching the transition, I pulled out my temporarily dry cycling shoes and socks, put them on, along with my helmet and "rain" glasses, and I was on my way.

I decided I was going to push the bike portion fairly hard since it was only thirteen miles. I did have to make adjustments on some of the turns, lest I crash my bike and lose layers of skin to the road. I managed a decent ride and was ready to run.

*Second Transition* (T2): I found my running shoes…still nice and dry, and neatly packed in a plastic bag I might add. I discarded my cycling gear, grabbed my running gear, and was off and running. Or was I off with my running? I headed to the wrong side of the tree which was where the exit shoot was. There were well-intentioned people yelling instructions at me like, "*Hey! A;hgiyhquao!*" Did you get that? Yeah, me neither. After I sorted it all out, I ran around the tree correctly and a kind volunteer held up the string of flags so I could run under them and get out on the run course. I'm sure it was quite a sight watching me play ring-around-the-bleepin'-rosy while I tried to get going on the run. Only slightly embarrassed, I was finally on my way. And yes, my running shoes were nice and wet already. At two miles I was feeling pretty good and knew I could hold my pace to the finish. I crossed the finish line and was pleased with my performance, despite the mishaps. I let the finish line volunteers know I was grateful they came out, and I walked away in my gray haze of having worked hard through water, and over hill and dale.

I had a good time, but I'm still not happy my bike got all wet. Ironically (and unofficially at this point), I was roughly thirty seconds *faster* than last year.

## The Great Buckeye Challenge ½ Ironman, August 2000 (1.2mi/56mi/13.1mi)

Though the race was in its first year, it was three years in the making for me. Ever since I saw Dai conquer the 1997 *Muncie Endurathon ½ Ironman*, I was inspired to do the same. However, it wouldn't be the Muncie event I would take on, but this type of event had been calling me. Courage, rather the lack thereof, lack of proper preparation, and time management difficulties kept me from attempting this distance for a year or so, but this year it all came together.

Race morning was a cool 60 degrees and foggy, but eventually the sun forced its way in and the day reached a warm-but-comfortable 75 degrees.

*The Swim*: It was difficult to navigate the 1.2 mile swim since spotting the marker buoys was nearly impossible with arms flailing, water splashing, and a thick fog. I hoped the people around me knew where they were going, so I stayed near them as we struggled to find our way around the swim course. I started the race safely to the outside, so if I had an "octopus attack," like at Clark Lake, I would have room to flop around grabbing my zipper while I recovered. Fortunately, I managed to keep the "octopus" off me. However, I found myself zigzagging and not staying on the rectangular, two-loop swim course, because sighting was a challenge. Eventually I came out of the water and felt pretty good. On to the bike!

*T1*: My wetsuit slid off quite nicely, I dried myself off the best I could, and then attempted to get into my cycling apparel. Typically I would not put on cycling shorts and a jersey, but considering the distance I would cover, it seemed like the right thing to do. My jersey and shorts clamped on to my wet skin while I attempted to slide them on. I had the sensation of putting on clothes that were my daughter Alex's size…what a pain. Ultimately I was dressed, on my Litespeed, and out of transition.

*The Bike*: The course description advertised for some rolling hills and some challenging hills, mostly in the first twenty miles. The day before the race we drove the first twenty miles to see what we would be up against. The hills were rolling and there were some challenging hills, so why not believe the rest of the course would be fairly tame? Well, we all know that to assume makes an ass out of you and umption. Sure enough, after twenty miles the hills just kept coming. Large hills, small hills, tall hills, short hills, curvy hills, straight hills, fast hills, slow hills. Basically we were living out a Dr. Seuss book about hills. The course description should have read… "Well, the last five miles aren't *too* hilly." At fifty miles into the fifty-six mile course I thought, "I would really like to get off my bike now." I thought better of it knowing this would only mean walking six miles to T2 in my cycling shoes. I remained steady and brought it home…and yeah, I even passed some people in the process.

*T2*: Not a big deal. I walked my bike in, discarded my cycling shoes, shorts, and jersey, along with my helmet and glasses, and threw on my running shoes and hat. Off I went. Ah yes, to prance around in multi-sport briefs was like nothing else. What other time can you run through a community in what appears to be nothing more than your underwear and not get arrested?

Knowing I've had a (self-diagnosed) chronic muscle tear in my right calf, and not having run for a week (minus two token miles the previous Wednesday to check my calf's progress) I was grateful for every mile God allowed. At mile one, after having been out on the bike for what seemed like a day, I had to go. I mean…*really* go! I shouted ahead to a race volunteer, "Is there a porta-jon near by?" He let me know the cornfield behind him had been the venue of choice for such things, and I didn't hesitate to take advantage. After peeing for what seemed to be several hours (a minute at most), I was on the road again, plodding along.

At mile two my calf still showed no signs of pain, so I thanked God. In fact, I thanked God after every mile I completed that day, because each mile was one more mile less I would have to walk in order to finish.

I walked through every aid station as planned, while consuming large quantities of water and Gatorade. I held my steady-but-slow pace, mile after mile. It seemed as though I was doing thirteen really slow, one mile intervals. I guess I was. At about eleven miles I began to grow weary and found myself walking when there was no aid station. I wouldn't allow myself to walk long though because heck, I was almost done!

With a half mile to go, there was an aid station. Well...I had to stop didn't I? That was the plan after all. I drank some water and carried on.

I could see the final 400 meters mapped out in front of me. My course was set: Across the grass, over the footbridge, over the parking lot, through the tunnel of flags, and through the finish line. I sprinted like a mad man, arms raised, and all the while screaming, "I'm the man!!! *I AM THE MAN*!!!"

...not really.

I trudged, dragging my depleted body over the remaining distance, and pressed "stop," on my Timex, Triathlon sports watch as I crossed the finish line in five hours and six minutes.

I thought I would be finishing closer to five and a half hours, so naturally I was thrilled with the result. I was so pleased I accomplished my goal that I was already thinking about my next half-Ironman adventure. "Hell," I thought, "I'll just jump back in the water right now!" Ok, I was excited, but not that excited. My hips were aching, my quads and hams were sore, and I had a blister on my heel. The only place I was going was to the massage tent, followed by the food line. So I can't claim that I became an Ironman, but I was now halfway there.

## Reeds Lake Triathlon, September 2000
### (.5mi/18mi/5mi)

Hmm. Not much of a story for this race. It was pretty normal-ish, and unfortunately that was the tone throughout the race, which was somewhat of a let down. I was calm before the start, remained calm through the swim, bike, and run. I was not emotionally charged; in fact I felt flat pretty much the whole race. One goal I had was to cycle really well, and I managed only a minute faster than my previous best here. That's something I can take from this I suppose. My run was strong, but uneventful. I was alone after the first mile, and it seemed as though I was running during somebody's cycling event (other competitors still in the cycling phase kept going by on the bike course which is on the same stretch as part of the run). My time was five minutes faster than 1996, which I am happy about, but the event itself seemed quite anticlimactic. Unless I am doing the event with friends, or I am totally focused on this event for some reason, I don't see myself doing it next year. My next event is the *Steelcase Grand Duathlon* where my goals are to race well, safe, healthily, be mechanical-problem-free, and to bring home one of the coveted *Grand Duathlon, Steelcase Chairs*. I am looking forward to this event more so than I was the *Reeds Lake Triathlon*. I think I felt somewhat of an obligation to do Reeds because it is so local and popular. Oh well, not a complete bust, just no fire today. (*Note: The run was measured short this year*).

# Chapter Two: Race Fans 2001

## Lake Macatawa Triathlon, June 2001
### (.5mi/22.8mi/4.8mi)

After having "Runner's Knee" for much of the spring, I had not put much running mileage in, and was not feeling particularly fit. My cycling was going ok, and my swimming was ok, but in general I was not as fit as I was at this time last year. At any rate, I was at the starting line of the 2001 *Lake Mac-Tri-*, as we call it. I was nervous about having a panic attack in the water, similar to last year's season. I prayed that I would be able to just relax and swim like I know how.

*The Swim*: It started out as a "water run" since the water was quite shallow and we could make better time in this modality, even though we were in the water. I believed on some level I was cheating, but since I didn't get a good warm-up in, I figured this was it. Eventually I began swimming, and I felt fairly good about things at first. Not too long into the race I detected the beginning stages of a panic attack coming on. I told myself to relax and go with it, but the nervousness continued. I decided to be proactive and swim on my back for a couple seconds, to try to nip this thing in the bud. It seemed to work, and I was able to swim normally for the rest of the swim. My time was fifteen minutes and some change. This is not really a fast time for me for a half mile swim, but I decided it was fair. (It is possible the swim was slightly long, but I'm not going to count on this being the case). Regardless, I would like to see my half mile swim in the area of 13–14 minutes however, not in the fifteens.

*The Bike*: I was not sure what to expect. My knee had been tender on several rides leading up to this race, and I was feeling tentative before I even got started. I guess I was sort of sitting back to see what would happen. As it turned out, my knee ended up feeling pretty good, and I began passing people. So, I decided to push the pace a little to see how it would respond. I figured I might as well because I didn't know how long I would be able to run after the bike anyway. Because I pressed the pace, I was only passed by two people (who I later caught on the run). I'm happy with how the bike went, but of course I would have liked to have been faster.

*The Run*: I decided to take it out conservatively because of my lack of fitness, as mentioned earlier, and because I wanted to give my knee a chance. It turned out to be a wise choice. My run was less-than-blistering, but it got me to the finish area. Prior to "breaking the tape," I decided at the last minute to duke it out with the guy immediately ahead of me. I sprinted, not expecting him to respond, but he did and we went neck-and-neck toward the finish where he marginally out-kicked me.

*The Bottom Line*: I had a good time. I enjoyed myself and set a positive tone for my season. This race was basically a "feeler event" to see where I was. I discovered I was doing better than I thought, and that I should train on with confidence. I thank God for the blessing of being able to participate and compete in triathlon, and I thank Maggie for her support of my passion for the sport.

## Seahorse Triathlon, June 2001
## (2k/40k/10k)

The swim portion of the Seahorse went fairly well. I felt pretty confident throughout. I did have some moments of anxiety, but they were brief and I got past them. I was both pleased and disappointed by my swim split of 17:58, because for a 2k swim, this would make me a world class athlete. Before you rush off to call *Swimmer Magazine* however, please understand the advertised 2k distance was considerably short. This was particularly disappointing because I wanted to have a preview at this distance before my half-Ironman. So it goes…on to T1.

My first transition was fair. I didn't have a long wrestling match with my wetsuit, and I managed to get my bike quickly out, and without causing other bikes to dislodge and fall to the ground. Most people don't take kindly to having their $2000+ bikes tossed about like the parts for *Mr. Potatohead*.

The bike leg was quite interesting to me. Although this was only my second triathlon of the year, I chose to ride more aggressively. For one unfortunate soul, I was like a mosquito in a camper's ear. He kept trying to pull away from me, but I kept coming right back. The bike course consisted of two laps, and at the beginning of the second lap, Mr. Calves-the-size-of-Montana, put in a surge to try to squish the mosquito. At the moment it was effective, but I did not lose hope, nor did I lose my determination. As I continued to press on, the gap began to close between us, but I had difficulty getting as close as I wanted to be. In the last one and a half miles however, he started looking over his shoulder for me. After each time he checked for me over his shoulder, I would throw in a surge. So, each time he looked back he gave up valuable real estate to me. He went from having about a 400–600 meter gap on me to having about 25–50 meters on me by T2. I think he was annoyed that "the skinny guy" was keeping pace.

My second transition was pretty fast, but as I left for the run I couldn't help but to think I was forgetting something. It turns out I didn't, but I hated feeling this way while putting distance between me and the transition area, where anything I might need was sitting. Though I learned later, it *is* against regulations to run naked, so my feelings of forgetfulness weren't entirely unfounded, and leaving my clothes was not a good idea (just kidding).

The run went well. My hope was to hold a steady pace throughout. I passed several people, held on to my pace, and finished without having to hold anyone off at the end. The next competitor was about two minutes back.

Basically, it was a fine day, a fine race, and a good time was had by all.

## Great Lakes Championships Triathlon, July 2001 (.5mi/18mi/4mi)

When I got to the race I was in somewhat of a haze. Oh wait, so was everyone else. It was muggy, steamy, and threatening to rain on our "freak show parade". No matter. I found my number on the designated sheet, received my race packet, was numbered on my arm and leg like a member of the cattle community, and then I set-up my transition area. "No wetsuits today," the announcer reported, "the water is 80 degrees." I thought this was cool because most of my swims lately had been without a wetsuit anyway.

*The Swim*: No major problems…except one minor detail. The major buoys marking the swim course were orange. So what? Well, the swim caps my wave had on were orange. Each time I would look up to spot my direction, I would view a sea of orange. I figured what the heck; everyone in front of me must know where they are going, so I just stayed with the group. At one point I considered simply swimming around one of my competitors and returning to shore, but then there is the whole thing about being disqualified. Not having my glasses on during the swim would not be an exception to the rule about "keeping the buoys on my right at all times." Anyway, I swam a decent time and gained reasonable positioning in the race.

*T1*: All the wrestling matches were postponed to the next race where wetsuits are allowed, so I managed to get going on my bike quite quickly.

*The bike* went comparatively well. There was some light rain to contend with, but there weren't any technical turns on the course, so I was fine. I did manage to get myself "stuck" in a peloton (group of riders), which is against the rules. I was riding as hard as I could, but I could not pull away, and I found myself in the middle of the darn pack. I couldn't move left, right, or drop back, because there were riders everywhere! Finally I thought, "FINE, I will let you all go!" Not a very competitive notion, but it was the right thing to do. I coasted until they all went around me. I didn't let them go entirely however. I kept my legal distance behind the pack, so I could hunt them down on the run, like the dogs they were!…Well, not exactly, but I wanted no more of their "illegal" activity.

*T2*: Quick transition again. Hat and sunglasses not needed…fairly light, but steady rain set in. The run was a concern because I recently acquired either a muscle strain, or shin splints, after a hard training run, and then succumbing to the temptation to shoot hoops with my brother Andrew. (He beat me, but it was fun nonetheless). Anyway, I ran within myself, but with a fast enough pace to pass several people and manage a strong finish. Yes! *Kudos to Tim Stack who placed second overall in the Duathlon held in conjunction with the triathlon.*

## Mark Mellon Triathlon, August 2001 (1k/50k/10k)

Prior to the 2001 *Mark Mellon Triathlon*, I ran to Maggie's parent's house at a blistering pace. What first comes to mind is someone running rather fast but, the truth is…I got blisters. I was concerned about my well earned blisters giving me trouble during the run, so I armed myself with a bottle of *New Skin* and some *Sport Stick Band-Aids*.

*The Swim*: I started off conservatively and managed to work my way back to shore with somewhat of a steady pace. The story of the swim was my feet. Thankfully I am not referring to an irritated turtle snapping at my toes. Unfortunately, what I am referring to is my "extra-strong" band-aid working its way off my foot!

*T1*: With my wetsuit off quickly and my feet wiped off, I was ready to apply a fresh band-aid. First problem: I didn't set one out. Solution: Rummage through my bag like a crazy-man until I found one. Moments later I had one. Here's the thing. Band-aids stick to wet feet about as well as eggs to Teflon! After struggling a bit, I had thoughts any rational person in my panicked state might have… "Screw it, I'm goin'!" So without a band-aid, I left in a hurry.

*The Bike*: The first half mile of the bike I don't recall very well, because I was busy trying to sort through the curse words flying through my brain regarding my lack of band-aid on my blister. After I got through with that nonsense, I refocused because I had some serious cycling to attend to. I was passing people pretty handily and liking it. Eventually an acquaintance of mine, who used to be a bodybuilder and has more muscles than most people are allowed, cruised by (likely with a smile on his face) and provided me with token verbal encouragement. I wasn't flustered by this because, the dude can ride. However, seconds later a pack of riders (who I will call cheaters because well…riding in a pack during a non-drafting triathlon is cheating) went zooming by me like they heard a rumor that there was not going to be enough post-race food for everyone. So, I kept my legal distance behind them and had a conversation with myself about what I was going to call them when I passed them on the run. Later however, the pack had broken up somewhat and I made my move. I passed them and put the hammer down. This was none to soon I might add, because right after my breakaway we faced three major hills. This was an out and back portion of the race so, let's just say there were six major hills. Skinny-power did the job, and I managed to work my way past a few more people while making my way back to the transition area.

*T2*: No problems.

*The Run*: The question of course was "Would my blisters give me problems on the run?" I hopped and prayed they wouldn't, and God gave me the go-ahead. Despite feeling rather fatigued toward the end, I managed a decent run and finished in basically the same time I did last year (2:20:-and some change).

Relieved my blisters didn't cause me any troubles, and after discovering the food shortage rumor was only something I made up earlier in this account, I was happy to have completed yet another *Mark Mellon Triathlon*. I didn't receive any hardware for my efforts, save the finisher's medal, but I was able to smile on this day and think, "I love this sport."

## The Great Buckeye Challenge ½ Ironman, August 2001 (1.2mi/56mi/13.1mi)

I guess the story here is that, I don't have much of a story. The swim went well. I swam strong and confident throughout without incident.

*T1*: Smooth and fortunately uneventful.

*The Bike*: The bike course was a bit different this year, but the same in the way that the hills were still huge and plentiful. I don't have a computer on my bike, but I am fairly confident I reached upwards of 40 mph going down a few rather large and steep hills. I am also fairly certain I went *negative* 3 or 4 mph going *up* some of the large and steep hills.

*T2*: Again smooth and uneventful.

*The Run*: I suppose if there is a story it's here. I got off my bike still in reasonably good shape to go sub-5 hours, but I crumbled like a cookie in the clutches of *Cookie Monster's*, blue furry hands. By mile four I was seriously questioning whether or not I should even finish the race. I walked, ran, walked, ran, and continued in this manner for some time. I decided that as long as I could still make a choice about whether or not to finish…I should finish. Three miles out from the finish, I looked at my watch and thought, "Now, if I could just run the last three miles in under fourteen minutes, I could still break five hours." I almost laughed aloud after the thought, and it kept my spirits high while I experienced my meltdown. I was definitely in survival mode most of the run. It wasn't advertised as such, but the event turned out to be a swim/bike/jog/walk/walk more/consider crawling/don't die event. I guess that would make it a heptathlon.

I finished in a disappointing 5:19-something. Last year I finished in 5:06-something, and as I noted earlier, I was shooting for a sub-five hour finish. I am only slightly disappointed however, because I had a decent swim and bike effort, and I enjoyed the challenge *The Great Buckeye* offered. HOWEVER, after finishing I began re-evaluation of my "intentions" to complete a full Ironman in the next five years. If the half kicked my butt this badly, I am not confident enough that a full Ironman is in my best interest. I guess for now, I will take last year's half and this year's half and call it a full! I don't have plans to return to *Buckeye* next year, and I may not do a half-Ironman next year at all. Nevertheless, the experiences have been great so far!

## Niles Triathlon, September 2001
## (.5mi/17.5mi/5mi)

After my ½ Ironman, I was pretty wiped out. I took a couple of days off and began light training. I continued to train with pretty low intensity and low volume. I decided that less would be more going into my final triathlon of the season. The morning started out dark, as it often is before 5:00 a.m., and it was a chilly 52 degrees out. I don't know about you, but when the air temperature is only in the 50's, it doesn't exactly scream out, "Hey, let's go swimming!"

We arrived with plenty of time for me to set-up and frequent the porta-jon. Since I didn't have my snowmobile suit handy, my wetsuit had to do. I walked down to the beach with Maggie and Alex, and I couldn't seem to stop repeating the phrase, "I am *crazy*." Maggie's response was "No, you're not honey; you're just stupid is all." Ok, she didn't say that, but she might have thought it. Anyway, I wasn't really afraid of the water being cold; it was the air after getting out of the lake wet that had me nervous.

*The Swim*: I placed myself far to the left to have lots of room to swim and to be free from too many flailing arms, legs, and other things that might flail. I started out steady and within myself, and I built speed as I went. After having done a 1.2 mile swim two weeks prior, this swim seemed short. When I saw the shore I got fired up and increased my pace, concentrated on good form, and to my delight, I noticed I was passing people. At last, I reached the shoreline. I decided it was just too dang cold out to expose myself to the air. I noticed other athletes around me also staying put. We all just sat in the comfort of the warm water. Ultimately the race director threatened, "Ok look people, if you don't get out of the water, you are all disqualified." We all just kinda' looked at each other and shrugged. The headline in the local paper the next day read, "Swimmers Refusal to Exit Water Cancels Niles Triathlon". That would have been funny, but it didn't happen that way. What really occurred was that I got out of the water and found the air wasn't as cold anymore. I hit the transition fast and furiously, and headed down the road on my bike.

*The Bike*: I decided to hammer from start to finish. It seemed to be working fine, as evidenced by passing about five people in the first one and a half miles. Was I afraid of blowing up on the run? Yeah, a little bit, but I thought, "Screw it, I'm goin' for it," and I did. Eventually I was passing a few more people, and only being passed by one guy, who I caught later on the run. The transition was seamless, and with my Saucony dogs on my feet, I was ready to run.

*The Run*: The air was crisp and cool and memories of cross country were prevalent. I found a steady pace to settle into, and I willed myself to maintain it for four miles. With a mile to go, I gradually increased my pace and found the gears I needed for a powerful finish.

It was nice having a strong race for my last triathlon of the season. I felt good about the race, and about myself. I don't know my splits or my place exactly, but I do know my time was a Personal Record (P.R.) for this course by one minute. I think I placed in the top 12–15 overall. As far as my age-group…hmm, look at it this way, the top eight were *all* in my age-group. Sheesh!

I hope you enjoyed sharing my triathlon journey this year. Party on…I'll be back next season!

**2001 Season End Notes:**

*Michigan Grand Prix Series*: 6TH OF 200+ (30–34 AGE-GROUP).

*USAT, Mideast Region—Honorable Mention, All-Regional*: (MICHIGAN, INDIANA, KENTUCKY, ILLINOIS, OHIO): 25TH OF 155 (30–34 AGE-GROUP).

*USAT, National Rankings*: TOP 22% (AGE 30–34 AGE-GROUP).

# Chapter Three: Race Fans 2002

## Seahorse Sprint Triathlon, July 2002
## (.5k/20k/5k)

Once the dust settled it all came down to Section 5.9 (b), of the *USAT Rules of Triathlon*. It was a day to test the waters post-surgery. For those of you who don't know, I had surgery to release my anterior compartment in my right leg, as a result of compartment syndrome. This was my first triathlon of 2002, and my first event of any kind since the end of my 2001 season. I chose to do the short course triathlon in Kalamazoo. The *Seahorse Triathlon* short course consists of .5k/20k/5k, swim, bike, and run respectively. The swim went well. No incidents of goggle stripping, elbow pummeling, or panic attacks. I felt quite good about the effort.

*T1*: Suh-low! It seemed like an eternity putting my dry socks on my damp feet. Try it some time when you are in a big hurry, and you will better understand the stress it can produce. I believe I was roughly fifth out of the water and third out of transition.

*The Bike*: After exiting the park and heading west down the road, I saw two gentlemen in front of me and in front of them was a vehicle with flashing lights. My first thought was "No way, that can't be the pace vehicle. Where is everyone else?" My second thought was "If there is nobody else, than let's go get 'em!" I pushed the pace and passed my first adversary. It turns out he was just a really good swimmer. The leader was in my sights, and I was closing in on him when some thick-legged cycling-type decided to crash my party. He passed me, and I passed him back, and then he took over our battle again. While we were playing cat and mouse, we managed to catch and pass the leader. Our bikes screamed down a super long hill, which we hammered relentlessly. No coasting here folks. Of course once at the bottom, while we were on a brief flat, the former leader passed me putting me into third position. We then had to pay the necessary dues for going down hill. Naturally this meant…going *up* hill. The hill was long and drawn out, but I kept my bike in a relatively low gear and spun my way up. After the hill, we raced across mostly flat terrain with occasional rolling hills. I noticed the leader, the runner-up, and I were basically traveling at the same pace, but in different spots. I put in some surges to close the gap and ultimately I found this to be effective. Within the last two miles I moved into second position. However, apparently not finding this particularly pleasing to the former runner-up, the guy made a move to take back the spot he believed to be his. Therefore, we all entered the transition area on our bikes in fairly close proximity.

*T2*: Much better. I discarded my shoes, helmet, glasses, and bike. After strapping on my running shoes, hat, and race number, I was out in short order. My competitors managed equally efficient transitions and we all left together. Within a half mile the leader was passed by the guy who was in second. I knew that had to hurt, so I made *my* move. I increased my pace in attempts to ruin his day early in the run. A few moments later I was the lead hunter. I was looking straight ahead for the leader and was intent on consuming the gap he established between us, but he was nowhere in sight. Apparently while I was passing the bike leader, the new leader decided that kickin' butt felt good, so he started kickin' mine. I never saw him again. I eventually cruised into the finish and held on to second place.

Satisfied with my results I took a casual swim with Alex, Maggie, and Claudia. Later I looked at the results to see if my Timex time matched the official results. They matched, but I noticed what I thought was an error. The score sheet read, "Sprint Overall Male Winner, Sam Wilkinson." I thought there was going to be an embarrassing moment at the awards. "Thank you for clapping, but, I didn't win. I was smoked by almost two minutes on the run by...insert name of guy who smoked me on the run by almost two minutes." However, as it turned out, the former champion failed to buckle the chinstrap on his helmet prior to exiting the transition area. He was told to stop, dismount, and clasp his strap, but he chose to clasp it on the fly. If he had stopped and followed the directions given by the official, he would have been fine, minus a time penalty, because they would have considered him "in transition". Incidentally, he chose to rock on and he paid the price. He was disqualified from the event per *USAT Rule 5.9 (b)*. It basically says you need to wear a helmet that has a stamp of approval. Furthermore, you need to have it on anytime you are riding your bike.

In short, though I was beaten by nearly two minutes, I became the *2002 Seahorse Sprint Triathlon Champion*. This was not as thrilling of a victory for me considering the circumstances, but I took the award home nonetheless.

A special thanks to Dai who sent me the bitchin' HED 3 wheels which had me lookin' sweet, cruisin' fast, and makin' a cool sound. *Excellent!*

# Traverse City Triathlon, July 2002
## (1.5k/40k/10k)

Currently I am somewhat uninspired by my *Traverse City Triathlon* perform-ance from this past weekend. I'm not sure what to attribute it to, but I have a few theories. One reason may be that I have yet to see the official results and don't know how I did in relationship to others. Another reason may be that I raced a bit conservatively on the run, and therefore, to some degree raced uninspired and out of the hunt. Lastly, it may be due to the fact that the tri-world regulars I have become familiar with were not present. It's hard to say, and frankly I don't know if it matters. Ultimately, it was a positive experience and that's what's important.

*The Swim*: The swim had a mass start, and though I am not generally a fan of such things it went quite well. One strange experience I had while swimming in the crystal clear water of the East Bay of Traverse City, was that I could see the sandy bottom the entire swim! It only got as deep as 10 feet or so mind you, but it made me painfully aware that when I travel by water, I only cover ground at about two miles per hour. The swim seemed quite slow as a result of this interest-ing perspective.

*T1*: I *meant* to bring a water basin of sorts for dunking my sand laden feet prior to drying them, and then shoving them into my socks. Because I didn't, I took advantage of those who did. As I rounded the first turn into transition, I noticed a small bin of water belonging to another participant...*left foot dunk!* As I entered my bike corral, I spotted another bin...*right foot dunk!* Feet clean! I managed to get out in decent time and with clean feet to boot...or shoe.

*The Bike*: I decided I would hit the cycling portion pretty hard. I didn't know when my leg (anterior compartment) might start to flare up, and so I didn't put a lot of stock in my running ability, and put most my eggs in my proverbial cycling basket. I had been cycling well lately, so I continued to put it to the test. I passed several good swimmers right away, and then as the bikes began to thin out, I caught a person here and there as the course progressed. It was quite a hilly course with some gorgeous views of the bay, which you could be DQ'd by the *Pay Attention To Your Surroundings Police* if you didn't take notice. The final uphill was the steepest. I'll tell you what; I did everything I could to keep from going backwards. After getting to the top, I was rewarded with a fast descent which required a sharp-ish turn at the bottom. Fine...slow down. I did slow down, but a few victims, who I did not witness, did not and they paid the price. They crashed their bikes and burned their hips while skidding across the pavement.

*T2*: I approached the next transition and noticed the athletes in font of me crossing the timing mat without getting off their bikes. I followed suit, but heard a man shouting, "If you don't walk over the mat, you won't get a time." All I heard was "Blah, blah, go back over the mat, because you don't want to end up like the guy who got DQ'd at your last race for not listing to a race official." So, I quickly ran back (about six feet), stepped on the mat, heard the chip sound, and continued to rack my bike. I was out on the run in quick time.

*The Run*: As I was running out, I felt some minor and brief hints of discomfort in my leg, so I backed off, settled into an easier pace, and held that pace throughout the run. I thought better of trying to hammer the run with the potential consequence of giving up my half-Ironman appearance toward the season's end.

After a conservative run, I was pleased with the outcome for the most part, and enjoyed the rest of the weekend camping with Maggie, Alex, Claudia, and my brother Joe.

*Special Note*: Again thanks to Dai for the bitchin' HED 3 wheels that assisted me in crankin' on the bike, and a special thanks to Mark Roach and *Gazelle Sports* for hookin' me up with the smokin' *TYR* tri-suit that dazzled any on-lookers, most of whom wondered how the clothes stayed on my skinniness. Moreover, thanks to Maggie and Joe for caring for our youngsters while I was out playing.

## Great Lakes Triathlon Championships, July 2002 (.5mi/18mi/4mi)

A little over 450 athletes prepared to throw their bodies into the murky waters of Gun Lake, as the haze from humidity settled in the area. This was a far cry from last week's episode where seeing the bottom of the lake was a normal thing. Gun Lake's mud-churned water allowed for zero visibility in the water. Nonetheless, the non-wetsuit swim (the water temperature was 80 degrees, and 78 degrees is the cutoff), went well as I made my way through the crowd of fellow age-groupers. My mind was not focused on the swim however, I was already thinking about the bike. I had it in my brain that the bike portion would be my time to shine.

*T1*: No troubles to speak of here. Although the wrestling match with my wetsuit was called off, it was still *on* with my socks, but it wasn't too much of a struggle.

*The Bike*: I started to take the bike leg by storm. I began passing people immediately and kept looking forward to overtaking my next pursuant. The hills were familiar from having trained on them occasionally, but they didn't give me any points for being previously introduced. While approaching the first of two turnarounds, I could see the "real men" and their mighty steeds fly by in a blur. I took a brief moment to acknowledge their greatness with words of encouragement, and then moved on inspired.

Returning from the first turnaround, I traded positions with an equally qualified adversary, but won the battle and moved on to the next. I was still passing those who established themselves earlier with a solid swim. Apparently the focus they had in the water was better than mine, since my focus even during the swim, was on the bike.

A couple years ago, it used to be that I would have a decent swim and cruise on the bike, only to be passed by many talented cyclists. Over time, that changed to a handful of cyclists passing me, and then later only a few passed me. Today's goal was to have nobody pass me. Well…I got passed. Ok, twice. However, I managed to reel both back in, and was able to obtain my goal. I had a satisfying ride. It appears that it was one good enough to write home about.

*T2*: I think this is the transition I have down to a science. Quick, smooth, and out.

*The Run*: I started out a little slow, but I progressively got faster as the race continued. It was an out-and-back with a few challenging hills, but no will-killers. I managed to pass more people on the run, and was able to keep all my pursuers behind me. Most importantly, my leg didn't bother me which was a relief.

I pulled off a strong finish, and I walked away with a grin while I headed for the aid station, after finishing. This is a great sport.

## Paul Bunyan 1/2 Ironman Challenge, August 2002 (1.2mi/56mi/13.1)

*Dedicated to the memory of Cailin Marie Hannebohn, a former student of mine who died unexpectedly from a cerebral aneurysm, at age 8.*

The first time I did a half-Ironman I *hoped* to go under five hours, but I hit 5:06. The second time I confronted the distance, I *tried* for sub-five hours, but I landed hard on 5:19. I guess the third time is supposed to be a charm. I traveled to a new venue, again with hopes of having a good go of it, and with dreams of obtaining the ever illusive sub-five.

Michigan's first ever half-Ironman distance triathlon was held in Oscoda, MI, on a course and day set for personal records. New roads had been installed in the last three years, and though cloud cover was abundant, there was no threat of rain. Early temps were in the upper 60's, with mid-70's the expected high, and little-to-no wind. Combine the aforementioned with a flat course, and you have a recipe for speed.

Roughly 200 men and women donned their neon green swim caps in the cool waters of VanEtten Lake. I strategically, or maybe fearfully, chose my starting position near the outside. It wasn't that I didn't enjoy the company of the other competitors mind you, it's just that…ok, I knew I wouldn't enjoy their company.

The event started close to the 7:30 a.m. scheduled time, and we were off to do battle through water, while rolling over hill and dale, and with one foot in front of the other. I started out conservatively to avoid getting my heart rate up too high, thus triggering a panic attack, and in order to get into a comfortable rhythm. As the swim continued, I gained confidence along with speed, and progressively made my way into the thrashing mass of people to take advantage of their draft. I came out of the water several minutes faster than previous years, and was only slightly surprised because, I knew I had put in a respectable effort on the swim.

*T1*: This transition generally takes a little time. Usually I get it right, but this time I made a minor error, but I didn't realize it until about 45 seconds into the bike.

After my shoes were clipped into my bike I was off, and I heard my supportive crew (Maggie, Alex, Claudia, Maggie's sister Britt, and her husband Joel), "Go Sam!" It was great to hear, but something wasn't quite right. At that moment I realized my error in transition. I had failed to take my earplugs out. I shook my head and smiled a little, as I reached up and took my plugs out, and put them in the back pocket of my singlet.

Kevin Miller is one of the best triathletes in our area, and when I discovered I was cycling near him, I knew I was doing just fine. At this point my goal was to try to hang with him. I figured why not, I didn't know what the run might bring, and I had put in my time on the bike… "Go for it," I thought. As it turned out, I hung with him for most of the bike leg before he remembered who he was and dispelled some dust in my direction (no offense taken). The final quarter of the bike leg I went back and forth with the women's leader. It wasn't that I couldn't stand being passed by a woman; it's just that I went faster on the flats and down hills. She was a scrapper, tough as nails, and ultimately, I didn't mind that she kicked my *a#$* when the fat lady sang whatever it is she sings when it's over.

*T2*: A little slower transition for me than a normal T2 because I was more tired than usual. My hamstrings were also tighter than what I generally experience at this point in the race.

*The Run*: With cautious optimism, I started the run. I had some minor shin discomfort during my last long training run, so I was monitoring my leg carefully. Last year at the *Great Buckeye Challenge ½ Ironman* in Ohio, I decided to walk at every aid station. This year I chose to simply run a steady, comfortable, and controlled pace, for as long as possible without stopping. I know, it sounds like an obvious strategy.

The run took us along part of an old Air Force Base, and then into a wooded trail nearby. The trail was 6 miles of the run, which was a benefit for me, because I was right at home in cross-country mode. At mile six I decided it was time to take a brief walk break. I consumed a *Carboom* energy gel, which the race volunteers provided, and walked for about 20–30 seconds before getting it together enough to move on. After this, I continued to have these brief walk breaks at each mile. The breaks were much briefer than at last year's *Buckeye Challenge*. Looking at my watch at every mile marker, I didn't pay attention to how fast I was going as much how much time I had to cover the remaining real estate. The sub-five hour barrier was doable, and I basically had to just keep moving to keep it within reach.

With three miles to go, my body really started to resist what my mind was asking it to do. My quads protested and went on strike, the blisters on my feet warned me not to go on like this all freakin' day, and my body was asking for fuel. My pace had dramatically dropped off and I was in survival mode. "Let's go! *You can do this!*" I told myself. While running I played the traditional mantras, such as "I think I can, I think I can, I think I can…" It sounds absurd I know, but it worked. Upon reaching mile twelve, I roughly calculated in my hazy mind, that I needed a ten minute mile to pull this off. A ten minute mile may sound easy, but when you are carrying quads that feel three times their weight, and you are fighting the urge to just sit down and call it a day in the middle of the street, a ten minute mile can be a battle. "Keep moving! C'mon!" my mind kept providing ammunition to grapple with my body, and it was prevailing.

Hardly soon enough, I could see the finish line shoot about 600 meters away, just around two turns. As I was plodding down the final stretch, I knew I was going to make it. My support crew was shouting encouragement as I approached the finishing shoot, and I was temporarily energized. Crossing the finish line was a relief, crossing the finish line was the goal, crossing the finish line under five hours was the dream, and now it was the reality.

Though it would have been more fulfilling to crack five hours at the more demanding course of the *Buckeye Challenge*, I took my time, recorded my results, and am proud of my efforts. I also took my race number to a young girl's grave. This one was for her.

*Time*: 4:53:00.

**1985 Caledonia
Cross Country**
*From left to right:*
Tim Hodgkinson,
Mark Cherpes,
Jeff Groendyke
Sam Wilkinson
Jeff Pierce

**1988 OK Gold
All-Conference
Cross Country**
*Left to right:*
Dai Wessman
Andy Lillie
Sam Wilkinson
Tim Hodgkinson

**1995 My Wedding**
*From left to right*: Mark Roach, Tim Hodgkinson, Sam Wilkinson, Andy Lillie,
Dai Wessman

**1998 Three Rivers Triathlon**
*Left to right*: Dai Wessman, Sam Wilkinson, Tim Stack

# 1995 Mark Mellon Triathlon...

## My First Triathlon!

Top: **2004 Lake Macatawa Triathlon** *Swim*
*Upper left*: Sam Wilkinson

Middle: **2003 Paul Bunyan ½ Ironman**
***Bike***
*Left to right*: Sam Wilkinson and
Kevin Miller

Bottom: **2005 Waterloo Triathlon** *Run*
Sam Wilkinson

**2004**
**Mark Mellon Triathlon**
**Triathlete at Five**
*Center:* Alex Wilkinson

**2005**
**Waterloo Triathlon**
**Two of My Biggest Race**
**Fans**
*Left to right:*
Claudia and Payton
Wilkinson

**2003 HFP Technica Adventure Race**
*Brothers*
*Left to right*: Tim Wilkinson, Andrew Wilkinson, Joe Wilkinson,
and Sam Wilkinson

# Chapter Four: Race Fans 2003

## 5/3 Riverbank Run, May 2003
### 25k Footrace

I don't recall my quads being quite so sore after my events last year, but it *has* been since September since I last competed.

The 26th running of the *5/3 Riverbank Run*, in Grand Rapids, Michigan was held May 10th, 2003, where close to 4000 participants put one foot in front of the other, to be a part of a grand tradition. The course followed the Grand River then wound runners through the urban streets to the heart of the city, where they finished at Calder Plaza. The course covered 25K (15.5 mi) of mostly flat road, with several rolling hills through miles eleven and twelve, and a couple small hills toward the finish to keep the runners honest.

I approached this event in the spirit of enjoying a long training day with thousands of other runners, who would politely escort me along the way. I felt no pressure to run a certain time, or to place anywhere in particular. I decided to just take it out easy, and let the race decide where I went from there.

The mass of humanity snaked through downtown and out toward the river's banks (thus the name), and it never really thinned out for many miles. The first mile for me was around 7:09. Ok, a *little* fast; I was figuring on about 7:15, but I decided to go with it because I was feeling relaxed and quite comfortable.

The first miles went by quickly, but not because I was running especially fast, but because I was running at ease, and there was a lot to take in. There were things to look at, listen to, and occasionally comment on to a fellow runner.

I noticed my splits were getting a little faster every mile, but not dramatically. I was feeling good and I didn't see any reason to fix what wasn't broken, so I just kept going with the flow.

Around halfway I was beginning to feel a little fatigued and slightly out of rhythm, but still felt like I was running well within my capacity. I had to wonder however, when my body was going to let me know it was not up for going at this pace.

While making a turn at the bottom of a hill, and transitioning to go up another, some kind souls had two very large speakers that blared out the tail end of Motley Crew's *Kickstart My Heart*. At one time, this was a fire-up song for me and my body gave me a shot of adrenaline. I guess the tune still did it for me. The song which followed was one I don't know the name of, but I know all of you know it. When hearing it I had a silly grin on my face and was jammin' in my head. It propelled me up the hill like it was a speed bump. *"I don't wanna' work, I just wanna' bang on my drum all day…"* Of course this song stayed in my head for the next couple of miles, and it was welcome.

Entering the infamous Butterworth Hills, (a series of hills beginning around eleven miles for about a mile or so) I was inspired by the fact that I was still feeling reasonably decent and I was passing people on the way up.

After the hills, I entered the city and subsequently *John Ball Park Zoo*. This is where my biggest fans awaited me. I arrived at the park to the chant of "Go Daddy go! Go Daddy go!" from Maggie, Alex, Claudia, and I am likely mistaken, but I thought I saw a rhythmic kicking of a baby's foot beating against Maggie's interior. Needless to say, it was inspiring with two and a half miles to go.

At this point, I was really starting to feel the race asking me to pay the toll. Yes, it's all fun and games until you start to feel the hurt. The first few miles of the race went by like they were only half miles. From miles 13 to 14, the stretch seemed like *two* miles! Consequently my thoughts went something like this, "Shouldn't there have been a fourteen mile marker around here by now…I could really use a fourteen mile marker…Did I miss the fourteen mile marker, because it should have been here by now…Hey where's the *freakin'* fourteen mile marker!!!"

Finally, the fourteen mile marker revealed itself and internally I did a little celebration dance. Here's the thing, apparently the event coordinators thought it would be funny to make the *"One Mile To Go"* sign three miles away because daaaaaaang-it-all, it took a long ass time for the fifteen mile marker to come into view.

At this instant, an angel appeared on my right shoulder and said, "You've come all this way feeling good, you will probably have a decent time, so just keep movin'." Of course hearing this, a devil emerged on my left shoulder and retorted with, "C'mon, you're just doing this for fun; as training right? Walk, relax, talk to the volunteers at the aid station for a little while." You have seen *Bugs Bunny* before, so stay with me here. "No, just keep going, it isn't that far. Slow down a *little* if you want, but do *not* stop. Go! Go! Go!" was the angel's rebut. "Walk just a little, that guy up there is doing it, and he seems to be better off," pleaded the devil. "For the love of Peter, Paul, and Mary…Go!" And the angel got the last word.

I continued on, gave a high five to a lady sporting an oversized, purple, foam hand, waved at a three-year-old-looking boy who was clapping, delivered my friend Marnie (Reynolds) a high-five, and approached the final curve before the finish.

There was an incline just before the final stretch that I had to conquer, (more race director humor) and at the peak of the hill there was about seventy-five yards remaining. Foolishness overcame me, and I ripped off my shirt like I just won the freakin' *World Cup Soccer Tournament*, and waved it above my head. I held my shirt in the air which read, "Lee Elementary" on it, with the signatures of the students at my school who had qualified for the *Jr. Riverbank Run*, and I trotted to the finish.

I imagined people were saying, "Look at *that* guy," minus the part where they say, "Who is so damn skinny he's lucky the wind isn't blowing. How *does* he remain upright anyway?"

I crossed the timing mat, took my timing chip off, received my finisher's medal, grabbed some water, and there standing on the spectator side of the fence were my biggest fans, happy to see me. "Daddy," I heard Alex shouting, "Nice job!" Followed very quickly by, "Can you get me a popsicle?"

## Technica, HFP Adventure Race, May 2003
## (5 mile trail run, 10 mile mtn. bike, orienteering,
## .5 mile kayak, and special events)
### *Team Dust For Breakfast...*

The adventure race did not leave us wanting for more, because it was all we expected, and then some. The adventure did not actually start in Nelsonville. The adventure began with Joe and Tim traveling across the country to join Andrew and me, in Ohio. Joe drove from California, and Tim drove from Montana, and both of them met in Utah, before trekking over to Ohio, in Tim's truck. They arrived sore, tired, and ready to get out of the truck. They traveled about 35 hours one way, and yes they did get an award for it, in the form of a shower and a full-sized bed.

It was at the "*butt crack of dawn*," as it is affectionately referred to, when the alarm sounded. We scrambled out of bed, got our gear together, loaded in the van, which already had our mountain bikes in it, and rolled down the highway for forty-five minutes to Nelsonville. After preliminary preparations by the coordinators and athletes, the race was on. Teams were required to stay together, and we did stay together the entire event.

Tim set the run pace and he worked his *arse* off. I was so proud I was grinning like an idiot...this theme prevailed throughout. The trail had very sharp inclines, and declines to match. As a result of the recent heavy rains that had drenched the area for several days, the trail was a glorified *Slip-N-Slide*. Grabbing trees and weeds to either propel us up the trail, or slow ourselves going down the trail was the norm. Mud was abounding, and water was eminent. After hoofin' most of the trail, we trudged under a road via a culvert, we crossed a bridge, romped through more trail, and then found ourselves facing a river. Life jackets and encouragement were offered as we took the plunge into the frigid, steadily-moving river. The air temperature was about 58 degrees, and there was no steam coming off the water. After Joe leapt off a bank about 10–15 feet high, I followed and went under water, and I never did touch the bottom. My glasses stayed on my face due to the *Croakies* I had on, and my hat exited temporarily. Joe however didn't have the same luck. Incidentally, if someone finds a nice pair of *Smith* sunglasses in a river, stream, or lake in Southern Ohio, he would appreciate it if you would either use them and enjoy them, or send them to him.

We air dried as we ran down more trail. We then navigated another culvert, smaller this time, with lots of bending on our part, and finally we swam across a cold pond which marked the finish of our five mile run. Our transition from run-to-bike was fairly efficient, and we began our next modality.

The mountain bike course was revised due to the condition of the trails, and we took to the road. We cruised right along the best we could. The bike portion was only about 10 miles long, but it was one of the hilliest 10 miles I have ever covered. We reached upward of 40 mph while descending at different times. This is quite fast for a mountain bike mind you. I was nervous about Andrew because he seemed to scream downhill faster than any of us, and because of the earlier rain, the roads were wet, and there was loose gravel on the curves. Andrew may have raced to speeds of more like 45–50 mph. I on the other hand, applied the brakes regularly. This part could have been a *Fear Factor* event. We made it back in one piece and began the orienteering mode of our adventure.

The orienteering involved following a map to various check-points, punching our card with unique markings at each point, and then returning to the transition. The rugged run, and the challenging bike took a serious toll on Tim's knee, and we had to walk this segment. Meanwhile, other teams scampered among us like dear bounding over fields and through woods. After finding all of the check-points, punching our card, and walking about two and a half miles in the process, we made it back to the transition area. They instructed us to proceed to the kayak staging area by the river.

We arrived at the starting point for the kayaks, which was about a half mile hike, grabbed our kayaks (two-person; provided), and began down river. Due to the high waters, and the resulting flood watch, the course was altered and therefore was about three-fourths of a mile long, rather than the one-to-two miles as advertised. At the end of the kayak section, we dug in and scrambled up the muddied riverbank. When we were all up the bank with our gear, we carried our kayaks back to the starting point; about a half mile walk by land. Finally, we made our way back to the transition area.

The special events we were required to do were varied, challenging, and entertaining. We began with a potato sack hop. This was a sack race if you can imagine, around a circle roughly 50 meters in circumference. Joe and I began hopping while Andrew was getting a drink, and Tim was still climbing into is luxury burlap race get-up. Joe and I were most of the way done when we saw Andrew bounding like a friggin' kangaroo. His hops were about five feet per leap. It looked abnormal, amazing, hilarious, and yet…frightful. Yes, frightful because he was maintaining this feat and was gaining on us very rapidly. Joe and I made an unspoken decision that we would not let him beat us to the finish, so we gave it all we had…which amounted to about six inches a hop. Andrew had people on their feet cheering, hootin'-n-hollerin' really, and he nearly beat us…Nearly.

They sent us to the recreation center next where we climbed a 25 foot rock wall, which was cool. We then went back across the pond, which as I mentioned was quite cold, especially since we had been walking around, and our bodies' temperatures had cooled considerably. Immediately following the pond, we stood shivering while attempting to put together a two-foot tall human skeleton puzzle. Having completed that, we carried a pole on our shoulders along a path until we reached a barn. Here we climbed the inside wall, crawled on our hands and knees through a hay maze, walked across a plank to the other side, and climbed back down. Of course being wet and adding hay was like being tarred and feathered, minus the scalding death effect that goes along with it of course. We picked up our poles once again, and carried them to the designated area before running across the finish line, with a time of 4:04:48. Andrew crossed with a cartwheel, Tim with a limp, Joe crossed at Tim's side, and I brought up the rear, and crossed with that silly grin still stuck to my face.

For our efforts we went home with finisher's medals, a second place trophy for our division, t-shirts and event singlets, pasta and other eats, as well as memories for a lifetime.

Thank you, Joe, Tim, and Andrew for traveling across the country to be part of this excellent adventure with me. You rock!

## Ann Arbor Duathlon, June 2003
## (2mi/14mi/5mi)

My hope was to stay with the leaders during the first run, but I didn't expect to be the leader. We started down a long hill, and instantly I *was* the leader. I was running within myself, so I wasn't too concerned about my pace being too fast. Looking at the field of competitors prior to the start, I expected them to be fleet of foot. We took to the trails a little less than a mile into the run and stayed on the trail most of the time. Exiting the woods I led my competitors to the transition area to the familiar rhythmic chant of "Go Daddy Go! Go Daddy Go!" from my supporters.

*T1*: Reasonably quick. Made a mental note that I pulled too hard on the strap on my running shoe, and it came undone, which meant I would have to thread it at T2.

*The Bike*: The course consisted of a great variety of hills. There were not many flat portions. Basically we were going up, going down, or getting ready to do one or the other. The hills were not monstrous, but they were numerous. I maintained an average of 22 mph on the bike, which put me two minutes faster than my 2000 effort here. It was difficult discerning who was a triathlete and who was a duathlete because the two events were being run in tandem, so I just assumed everyone was someone I needed to catch, and I kept it on. With about three miles to go however, a fifty-year-old stud with calves that could take an eye out if you weren't careful, went by me. I knew he was in the top three at the end of the first run, so I stayed within eyesight of him through the remainder of the ride. Again I returned to the enthusiastic "Go Daddy Go!" cheers which always gives me energy.

*T2*: I had to fix the strap on my shoe, but it only took a couple of seconds. Then I couldn't find my hat, which was a disappointment, but I left it behind nevertheless.

*The Run*: The run course was 98% challenging trail. There were several quad-busting hills and some ankle grabbing ruts and rocks, but it was not a mud-fest, so all was good. However, I was a little nervous without my glasses because seeing the trail was difficult. Squinting took place when the trail looked a little treacherous. With about two and a half miles to go I came upon Mr. Calves. I decided to stay on his heals for a while to feel out the situation. I envisioned staying with him and then out-kicking him in the last quarter mile. However, I was making a little better progress than he, so I passed him going up a hill. I put in a big surge and put some space between us. It was a twisting and turning trail, and I was no longer in his sight. My hope was he thought I maintained the pace I carried when I passed him. The truth was I backed off and resumed my previous pace, but at this point I had a good idea I was leading the duathlon. I had to keep pressing because I knew this was no normal 50-year-old on my tail. When we broke the trail and took to the road, we had to conquer a sizable 200 meter hill. When I was about halfway up I saw my hunter on the road, and he could see me now too, and he looked determined to close the gap. I picked it up slightly, realizing he knew I was within his reach. I entered the park which took us down a hill toward the finish. I shouted in short burst to Maggie and Pete (Bodary), "Red, white, and blue…Red, white, and blue…how far?!" I heard Pete respond with, "About 200 meters!" I went to the next gear and continued my trip down the hill. When I reached the last 200 meters I gave it everything I had left, crossed the finish line, and earned my first duathlon overall victory! Red, white, and blue guy, who I also referred to earlier as Mr. Calves was actually Mr. Dave Hines, and he finished not too far behind me in second.

The morning was thick and clouds were heavy, and after I finished I rushed up to put my bike and gear in the van. When all was secure the sky fell, and the rains came tumbling down. We stood in the rain with umbrellas, and patiently waited while all the triathlon awards were given. After our long wait, they gave out the duathlon awards. I was hoping to walk away with a fleece vest like my friend, and former Caledonia harrier, Tim Stack earned when he won here three years ago, but I accepted my plastic trophy with pride, gathered the girls with Maggie, and drove home especially satisfied.

## Seahorse Triathlon, June 2003
## (1.5k/40k/10k)
## "Serious Play"

When I was a *younger* kid, Tom Pickard and I would play catch with a football. It was not uncommon for us to claim to be professional athletes to receive the respect necessary to carry out the fantasy of being significant players of the game. I generally claimed to be Lynn Swan, the legendary wide receiver for the Pittsburg Steelers. This way I could not only catch any ball that came to me, but I could catch it with style and grace, no matter that it was fabricated by my mind's eye. The drama of course involved diving or leaping for a ball that mere mortals could in no way retrieve. Naturally, my imagination had my leaps and dives worthy of awe from the large crowd on hand. Swan could do it, so I could do it…I was Lynn Swan after all. This was serious play.

*The Swim*: My swim was sufficient despite some goggle difficulties early on, and the fact that my earplugs were resting on the bathroom counter at home.

*T1*: I ran up a hill into the transition and I felt kind of funky. Feeling a little disoriented is normal to some degree when going from horizontal to vertical while exerting a lot of energy, but not to the level I was experiencing it. On this day, after I quickly dried my feet and attempted to put on my socks, I noticed the world was spinning very fast. I took a knee and "enjoyed" the ride for about ten seconds. When the whirling ended, I put on my cycling shoes, and other required gear, and was on my way with no further incident. Later I realized the episode was directly related to not having my earplugs in during the swim.

*The Bike*: The race venue had three events going on concurrently. This is commonplace when the events are a long distance triathlon, a short course triathlon, and a duathlon. Anyway, I did not know which participants were which, but I was passing many athletes on bikes and enjoying the heck out of it. Occasionally I would look at a cyclist's legs to see if he had a T, D, or an S, and his age. All of this was written clearly in marker on athletes, along with ones social security number, phone number, e-mail address, and number of triathlons completed so far this season. Ok, not really but, the event letter and age is generally noted during these events. I passed a whole lot of people in the first loop of the two-loop course, most of which were short course people. After the first loop, I continued to pass people, but not in the same rapid-fire manner as before. I was now gaining on the athletes who were doing the long course like me, and there is usually a deeper field of talent among these athletes.

As I was cruising along on my bike, I told myself I was a powerful cyclist, and that nobody had anything on me. To continue this role, I announced, though not to Tom Pickard, but to myself, that I was Steve Larsen. He is a former pro cyclist gone triathlete who has many of the best cycling times in triathlon. I powered forward with increasing confidence knowing those around me would be hard pressed to pass Steve Larsen. Again, this was serious play.

Nobody did pass me the entire time during the bike segment, and I finished strong and felt a certain amount of redemption for having only an adequate swim.

*T2*: Quick and to the point. No *Tilt-A-Whirl* ride this time.

*The Run*: It was a double out and back course. I knew once I finished my first 5k it would be mentally challenging turning around from the finish line, only to head back out for another dose. I started out relaxed and ran negative splits (increasing faster throughout the run). I had a solid finish and felt good about the day's effort.

Yes, the "Go Daddy Go!" brigade was on hand in full force, which was much appreciated. It was a great beginning to a wonderful Father's Day.

## Muncie Endurathon ½ Ironman, July 2003
### *U.S. National Long Course Triathlon Championship*
### **(1.2mi/56mi/13.1mi)**

Maggie and I traveled to Muncie, Indiana in the summer of '97 to watch Dai (Wessman) conquer the *Endurathon*. It was a clear, sunny, and about to be a hot day. The distances the triathletes covered seemed overwhelming, and the speeds at which they traveled while covering them was amazing.

The first triathlon I witnessed featured Dai, and I was inspired to get involved. The longest triathlon I observed once more showcased Dai, and again I was inspired to reach his level of achievement. After three half-Ironman events completed, and seven years in the sport, it was my turn to make my journey to Muncie. It was my time to experience first hand what I had only imagined as being a remote possibility in 1997. As it was last year, this year's Muncie played host for the *U.S. National Long Course Championship*, and that was icing on the cake.

Temperatures started out in the low-to-mid 60s, and although it was close, the temperature never exceeded 80 degrees. There was a wind, but it was nothing severe, and the day's conditions left it up to me to do my thing as a triathlete. It was a day set for fast times at Muncie.

Over 1,200 neoprene donned competitors from across the country were anxiously awaiting the start of the race. Fortunately, there were several wave starts to this event, because a mass start with this number of people would have been a strong deterrent from my entry in the first place. Each wave was separated by about fifteen minutes, and I was in the third wave.

*The Swim*: "Three, two, one!" the starter shouted, and then the horn sounded, followed by 132 males, ages ranging from 30–34 crashing into the water. Considering the small-ish number, there was plenty of space to maneuver and get into a rhythm early. I chose to stay a little to the outside in case I needed an escape. After I settled into a steady pace and my heart rate was at a level I was comfortable with, I worked my way back into the "school" of swimmers to gain any kind of drafting advantage I could. A little over thirty-four minutes later I was on shore and jogging up a long hill to the transition area. My swim was slower than last year's half-Ironman, but a respectable time nonetheless.

*T1*: My first transition was appropriately eventful with no major hang-ups to speak of. Well…I actually *almost* knocked over all the bikes on my rack, which would have meant certain death for me when the others arrived. I stumbled with my foot stuck in my wetsuit, knocked my bike the neighboring bike sideways. This caused them to sway, which would have created a domino effect with all the bikes on the rack if enough contact was made. In the end, the bikes stayed put, and I managed to pack my *Cliff Bars* in my jersey pockets, and took to chasing the white line on my bike.

*The Bike*: Early in the race we turned off the country roads we were traveling and on to a *Rails-To-Trails* paved pathway. It was blocked off to all other trail users, so oncoming traffic was not an issue. It was very cool being able to cruise so fast down a trail of this type. Using this thing as a bicycle expressway is usually frowned upon under normal circumstances. It often has children wobbling with training wheels, older people walking, and baby joggers being strolled by mothers and fathers, on an afternoon jaunt.

We later exited the trail and headed down a local highway. Those with long-time familiarity with the greater Caledonia-Middleville area will understand when I say, it was like M-37…the old one, with the bumps. I was passing many people early and my ego was inflating, but it had no grounds because the preceding wave consisted of the more, shall I say, senior competitors. One athlete I passed sported an "80" on his right calf. I was compelled to give him a thumbs-up as I went flying by, and he reciprocated. "All right!" he shouted, at the same time as my back wheel proceeded ahead of his front wheel.

When we began traveling north-northeast the wind asked for its toll for pushing us along the course thus far. The road too was beckoning for payment for being mostly downhill or flat, and the terrain became temporarily hilly. Fortunately for those hoping for a fast time, or for muscle recovery enough to have a decent run, this was the only set of hills of consequence.

The return trip was fun while it lasted, that is until we turned north again and battled the wind for another fifteen miles. The wind was not especially strong mind you, but it was definitely apparent. Around fifty-two miles my adrenaline or my *GU*, I'm not sure which, kicked in and I had enough energy to surge past a few more competitors before finishing the bike segment.

*T2*: It was clean with no problems. I traded my bike for my running shoes and headed out.

*The Run*: It started out well. I established a realistic pace that I believed I could carry the whole way. I decided at that moment, I would try to keep a slower pace and hope not to hit the wall so hard later in the run. I thought this would be better than cruising, hitting the wall, and struggling severely. Well, you know what they say about the best laid plans. At least for the *first* mile I still felt reasonably decent. I decided to walk briefly as I downed some water and *Gatorade*. I did the same at the following mile's aid stations, and I still felt under control and comfortable. Around four miles however, my shin flared up dramatically with sharp pain. I stopped to massage it a bit, but then I continued with cautious optimism, and the pain persisted. I thought I would have to ask for a ride to the finish line once I arrived at mile five. Strangely, only moments later it went away almost as quickly as it came on.

The run course was basically hilly the whole time. The hills were not huge, but they were uninterrupted. My mind began to wander and I started thinking about the rest of my season. I still had three duathlons in the *Michigan Grand Prix Series* I was hoping to do well in, and this was only my third multi-sport event this season. If I put it all on the line today, it could be the end of my season. These were not welcomed thoughts when I was trying to do well in Muncie. My focus should have been on the task at hand, but instead, I basically talked myself into wimping out. I continued to walk at every aid station, which was fine and also beneficial for getting fluids down, but then walking crept in *between* aid stations as well. To perform soundly at an event of this type, one needs to be strong in all facets of ones being. It's important to be on top of your game psychologically, emotionally, intellectually, as well as, physically. Because I allowed negative self-talk to drag me down to a point where I couldn't lug myself up, I had in effect bankrupt a potentially a stellar day at the races. I walked/jogged to the finish line. Of course I *jogged* the last 200 meters or so to cross the finish line…people lookin' and all, you know.

I didn't know what to expect while crossing state lines heading into Muncie. I was however, secretly hoping to match or surpass Dai's effort. His was a very solid 4:53, but I didn't come close. However, the event was not a bust by any means. I enjoyed the experience of taking on the challenging event. It was an honor being part of the *US National Long Course Triathlon Championship*, and it was cool putting in the work to get here. What can I say? I love this sport!

## Great Lakes Championship Duathlon, July 2003 (2mi/18mi/4.5mi)

Going into this race, I originally had hopes of winning it outright. I found myself overanalyzing things…big surprise here. I examined the previous year's results, the results of the other series events I hadn't competed in so far this year, and the list of competitors intending to toe the line at *Great Lakes*. I concluded from my "research" of people who might win, that there were many athletes who had the potential to take the top spot. I got to the point where I talked myself out of having a real chance of taking the overall prize. I decided I would hang on to the leaders the best I could, and stay optimistic about my chances of winning my age group.

The horn blasted down by the waterfront to start the first wave of the triathlon taking place the same time as the duathlon. This was when our starter shouted, "Go!" I took off with the idea that I would go fast enough to be with the principle group, but not so fast that I would be the leader. This turned out to be a good plan, and I kept the leaders in sight without taking charge too early. By the first mile I was in fifth place, but I was comfortable because I was still in striking distance of the lead group. I tried to run as relaxed as possible because I knew the first mile was basically a long gradual downhill. This tactic allowed me to have more energy for the return trip of the out-and-back course. My strategy seemed to work because without changing my effort much, I positioned myself in third place within a quarter mile of the transition, and less than a minute behind first place.

*T1*: This transition was pretty smooth and efficient. I boarded my rig and peddled strong in pursuit.

*The Bike*: After the transition, it became increasingly difficult to discern my place in the event because triathletes and duathletes were sharing the road. I could have maintained my position in third or lost some ground in the transition, but I couldn't make a determination for certain. Several duathletes were close behind me on the run and could have had faster transitions, and theoretically would have been in front of me somewhere. I just didn't know. This time on the bike my goal was to be strong and steady, but not to leave everything I had out on the course, and hope for fresher legs on the second run.

The wind picked up considerably when we started heading west, which was about three miles into the 18 mile route. The longest straightaway began at this point, so I knew I would be dealing with the headwind for quite some time. I maintained my tenacity, but only passed one or two people before the turn-around, and I still did not know my position in the race. When I approached the fifteen mile mark, I finally recognized the duathlete who was in second just prior to the end of the first run. I passed him prior to reaching T2. Here's the thing though, about three people passed me on the bike that I didn't recognize from the first run, and this meant they were possibly stronger cyclists than runners, or they were contenders in the triathlon. Either way, it left me more confused to where I was in the race. I knew I had to be in the top five or so, but nothing more.

*T2*: This was satisfactory even though I struggled for a moment with a strap on my cycling shoe, which reattached itself temporarily.

*The Second Run*: I was feeling reasonably confident, and I continued along with a respectable pace. I passed a few people before the first mile who I believed to be triathletes, and then kept pace behind a gentleman who was carrying my same tempo. Around a mile and a half, I put in a surge to pull along side this guy, and I stayed with him until about a mile to go. Through spurts of brief conversation, we determined we were both in the duathlon, we were not in the same age-group, and there were likely three, maybe four duathletes in front of us. He was similarly confused about his position in the race as I was. We were persistent with our reasonably swift pace as we took on thee rolling hills the course threw at us, and while approaching roughly the three and a half mile point.

I began to fizzle within the last mile. I probably had more in the tank than I gave myself credit for, but mentally I had conceded the race to the guy I was running with, and he commenced in pulling away (this is something I'll need to work on next race). In due course, he finished the duathlon in front of me earning second place overall, making me third. As it turned out, the fist place finisher was awarded $100, and the second place finisher $50. I finished with a time of 1:27:21, and the second place finisher scored a 1:27:12. Clearly I was not too far from a payday…but I blew it. Nevertheless, I did finish first among males 30–34 years old, and did have a positive experience. A few lessons were gleaned from today's event. First I learned not to psych myself out by overanalyzing. Secondly, I should not assume I am out of contention if I don't know. Thirdly, I can't be a wimp in the last mile, and finally, even if the guy in front of me is not in my age-group, I need to remain compelled to run him down. None of these are new lessons for me, but the experience allowed for a great refresher course in the obvious.

This event was particularly enjoyable for me given that it took place in my own community. I was fortunate enough to not only have my usual cheering contingent on hand, but also my Mom, Dad, Maggie's Mom and Dad, and special guests, visiting from North Carolina were Eric, Marcie, and Cole Seubring. This is without mentioning a host of people from our area.

## Mark Mellon Duathlon, August 2003
## (5k/50k/5k)

Here is the short story…

*First Run*: Pushed early to see what the rest of the field had to offer. A few responded, and we left many behind. After the reaction of the other runners, I settled back into fourth place or so, contented to only keep an eye on the leader.

*T1*: Went o.k. and I was on my way.

*The Bike*: The leader took off about twenty-to-thirty seconds before I did and created a surmountable gap, losing himself in the crowd of triathletes. I hammered the best I could knowing the leader was the winner of last week's *Great Lakes Championship* event, and I didn't know the ability of my pursuers.

*T2*: I quickly traded my bike for running shoes and put one foot in front of the other.

*The Second Run*: The leader was only about fifteen seconds ahead of me, but he looked a little stronger than I felt. I set out with a sound pace that I thought I could maintain. I held on and finished not far behind the champion. His time was 1:55:52, while mine was 1:56:48. The next finisher was ten minutes behind me. It was a cool and rare experience for me to be in a position where I was runner-up overall and where we demolished the field. I enjoyed the moment, because one like this might not happen quite like it again.

Following the event, fine food was served for the athletes and our families…a big draw for this event I might add. Camping was fun and the girls and Payton behaved reasonably well in our camping surroundings. The weather held out for us. There were storms all around us at different times during the weekend, but we seemed to be in a pocket of good weather.

Ali and Anisa (Shaw) competed in the kid's triathlon in the afternoon and they really seemed to enjoy themselves. Perhaps their experience will inspire them to continue to pursue this great sport.

## Shermanator Triathlon, August 2003 (1.5k/40k/10k)

If you really want to look good, go to a first year event held on the same day as an established event, occurring at the same time. Although my intention was to support a local event, the fact that the Sylvania, OH Triathlon was going on the same day didn't hurt my chances for placing well. The field of one hundred athletes was small for a triathlon. Some competed as teams while others put out a solo effort.

*The Swim*: The men started first, followed by the women, and then the relay teams. I began steady-but-cautious, not knowing what kind of swimming fitness I would have because it hadn't been much of a focus as of late. I settled into an honest pace early and gained confidence enough to pick it up and draft behind a fellow competitor. It turned out to be my best swim in a long time; certainly for this year…who knew?

*T1*: We ran up a small hill to the transition before losing our neoprene super hero suits and becoming cyclists.

*The Bike*: It started out on a hill, so athletes whose bikes were racked in a high gear struggled to get a good start. The course contained rolling hills and numerous turns, many of which were rather tight. I passed a few people and could see a van in the distance with yellow flashing lights. "No way," I thought in disbelief, "am I in the lead?" The answer was yes! I lead the race for basically the entire second half of the ride and I was hammering because I didn't know how long it would last, and frankly being a big dog was a good feeling. However, within the last few miles, I traded the lead with another competitor for the top spot. That is until the end where we entered T2 together.

*T2*: I quickly transformed into a runner and was the first one heading away from transition.

*The Run*: Immediately there was a steep hill, but adrenaline allowed me to power up quickly. I knew my friend Kevin (Miller) was in the race, and if he was anywhere near me on the bike, he was going to smoke me on the run. I didn't look back though, and enjoyed being the race leader…*how cool!* When I exited the YMCA race venue to the local road, I looked over my shoulder and saw a person only about 200 meters behind me. I didn't know who it was but, I hoped it wasn't Kevin. I figured if I could just hold on to the pace I had I could win, *if* I had a first-rate lead on Kevin. With a mile and a half down, I was still running solo. The second mile marker was rapidly approaching and I would soon learn that Kevin was too. He came up on my side and I teased saying, "I thought maybe you got a flat out there." He laughed as he cruised by me with his seemingly effortless gait. I followed up my teasing with encouragement, "Good job...bastard!" Oh, the "bastard" part was just in my head; no real ill will intended.

My party was now crashed, so I had to hold on to what I had. I kept Kevin in sight as we toured up and down yet another rolling hills course. I knew he was holding back, which was fine with me because he was pulling me along.

When we approached the last mile and entered the YMCA, I asked a volunteer, "Anyone back there?" I received the words I hoped for, "I can't see anyone." After a few more curving uphill challenges, we were fortunately able to run downhill to the finish. Kevin won by about a minute, but what the heck, I'll take second place.

According to the results, I had the seventeenth fastest swim split, the fastest bike split, and the second fastest run split. I am most pleased with my bike split. The bike is something I have really grown fond of in the last couple of years and so I am enjoying seeing improvements in this area.

# Chapter Five: Race Fans 2004

## Lake Macatawa Triathlon, June 2004
## (.5 mile swim/22.8 mile ride/4.8 mile run)

The morning of the 2004 *Lake Macatawa Triathlon* began with thunder and lightning, along with wind and rain, but fortunately things changed. The forecast had called for isolated t-storms at daybreak, so the situation was not a surprise. By the time we reached the lakeshore community of Holland, the thunder and lightning had subsided, the wind had mostly calmed, the rain which remained was light-but-steady, and the morning light was now apparent.

You know by now, that I hate it when my bike gets wet. I brought with me a *HEFTY, Lawn and Leaf* bag to cover my bike in transition. Luckily, by the time I was in the transition setting up the rest of my gear, (and putting it in kitchen trash bags) the rain diminished and only cloudy skies remained.

*The Swim*: The air temperature was about sixty degrees, and the water temperature was only slightly warmer. Fortunately I was placed in the first wave so I didn't have to remain shivering on the shore while others swam before me. After a ten second count-down and a shout of "Go," the purple swim cap wave I was in began. I decided I would approach each leg of the event the same. I chose to ease into each discipline and progressively gain momentum to a level I could tolerate and maintain. This race was basically serving as my gauge to see where I was with regard to fitness, and to see how my body would hold up.

Fear was not a factor for me. Spotting strange green objects that freak me out, like when I'm training in Bassett Lake, would be a non-issue at Lake Macatawa, because the water had the appearance of coffee with a lot of cream added. "Look, you can see the bottom," I said to a fellow athlete as we entered the water, "Oh nope, that's the top." Because of my easy-going start, I didn't jack my heart rate up too rapidly. I'm sure this prevented me from feeling as though my wetsuit was conspiring with the water to drown me. I began passing people one by one and little by little as I increased my effort and pace. After rounding the last orange buoy, which resembled a very large florescent marshmallow, I started sighting for the shore. I swam the rest of the way with a guy in a full-wetsuit, and I pondered whether or not he would be next to me if his wetsuit was sleeveless like mine, or if he would be just behind me. I ultimately exited the water and rushed across the sandy shore toward the parking lot to where my temporarily dry bike was awaiting me.

*T1*: No transition records were broken today. My wetsuit was almost all the way off when it decided to grab on to my right ankle, as if a last stitch effort to get me to take it along with me on my bike. Eventually I freed myself, and put on the gear I needed. While I was changing modalities, Maggie, Alex, Claudia, and Payton (a little flexibility with Payton here) shouted words of encouragement as well as the word "computer." I knew if they hadn't reminded me to start my cyclo-computer, I would likely forget to in the heat of transition, and not notice until a mile into the race, and then everything would be off. Finally, I mounted my titanium steed and began my pursuit.

*The Bike*: Again the plan was to start conservative and build. Before I got to the top of the first hill coming out of the transition, my tires were drenched and my white racing singlet looked as though its design was *mocha-dot*. As I gradually picked up my pace on the streets of Holland, I found myself passing people in short order. I was thinking, "Ok, it's cool. Just get the good swimmers first and work your way up." My shoes were soaked after about a mile but, learning from a previous mistake, I knew that shoe covers are a good idea when the temps are cool are a good idea. It was evident that I had caught up to the better riders when passing became more of an effort than before. The course is an out and back, so I was able to count how many were in front of me. The first eight athletes I usually give "props" to because I am fairly confident there is no way I am going to catch them. After this I will give a shout to those I recognize, and then I keep my mouth shut because the next ones are on my radar for consuming. I counted fourteen athletes before I hit the turn-around. I was in deliberate pursuit of the rider moving right along in front of me. He was a good seven-to-ten bike lengths ahead of me, and he wasn't gaining ground on me as we motored along. We began passing people and my re-count put me around eleventh (in my wave). When we were within four miles of completing our 22.8 mile trek, I sensed it was time to make my move. The guy I was shadowing started standing on his pedals while going up hills, and then I even saw him coast for a moment. If I had looked carefully enough, there might have been a sign at the side of the road reading, "*SAM, GO NOW!*" I don't think he realized he was being hunted for many miles and that I was about to strike. I passed him as we were going downhill and nearing an intersection. I dropped the hammer to make my pass decisive. As I moved alongside him I kept my eyes straight ahead and kept on crankin' like I never realized he was in the race. I'm sure he didn't appreciate being perceived as insignificant.

After all he had been hammering all the while being the passer, not the passed. I instantly put two-to-three bike lengths on him, and before he had a chance to respond it was time to turn at another intersection. After the turn, he wasted no time carrying out his obligation to show me his dominance and his resistance to being overtaken so easily. He went firing past me in the same calloused fashion I went by him. "Good for you," I thought, "but I'm not going away." He managed to gain five bike lengths on me, but we were going up a long gradual uphill, and I knew it would just be a matter of time before I caught him. He was struggling on the hills earlier, so I thought I had a good chance. I also figured me with my slight frame, and he sporting a bulkier model, that my body type was more suited for the next slightly hilly mile. I overtook him again, but this time I knew he was well aware of me, and his body language was much different on this pass. I sensed he knew I had him. His breathing was more labored and he slumped over a little when I went by... "Yes!" I thought, "Go!" I put in another surge and put a gap on him which he never recovered from. It was a cool engagement, but too bad it wasn't a battle for the win. Approaching T2 I saw the leaders running along the road, and they were already more than half a mile into the run. I took a bite of humble pie, but it didn't damper my earlier battle's victory.

*T2*: My now wet and sandy bike was quickly placed on the rack. I changed shoes, replaced my helmet with a hat, and left the transition behind me.

*The Run*: The theme of negative splits prevailed. This was especially timely because we had to run on a boardwalk for a short time which was rather slick from the rain. A slow-ish pace at this time was prudent. While going up the last hill before hitting the streets, I felt surprisingly good. I kept it on and held a steady pace, and found myself passing people once in a while. "Huh..." I thought, "Cool." Within a mile and a half of the finish, I caught a gentleman and thought I would try and hang with him. However, to get a feel for what I could do, I didn't pull along and adopt his pace; instead I surged slightly, found myself ahead of him, and pressed forward. He didn't back down and was right on my heels for about a mile. I didn't want to find myself in a sprint finish, so I increased my pace with a half-mile to go and managed to shake him before entering the finish at *Dunton Park*. I cruised down the hill along the winding path, held on down the grassy straightaway, and crossed the finish line feeling pretty good.

**Notes**: The swim was rumored to be long. Thank goodness. I didn't think I was that bad off. Furthermore, later waves had representatives who beat me to the finish, but I had a great day participating in a great sport. *My efforts in this event were dedicated to Eric (Seubring) who at the time was risking his life in Iraq so I could "play" here at home.*

## National 24-Hour Challenge, June 2004
## (As Far As You Can Ride In 24-Hours)

To win the 24-Hour Challenge you need to cover more ground on your bicycle than anyone else in 24-hours. Although there were many out on the course striving for the title of *National 24-Hour Champion*, I was not one of them. The idea of cycling for 24-hours is not an area in which I currently have an interest. My intention in entering the event was to complete the first of three loops. The first loop covers 126-plus miles, the second loop covers a little over 23 miles, and the third loop, the night loop, covers slightly more than seven miles (You do the first loop one time, the second loop as many times as you can with daylight, and the third loop at night as many times as you can). I was curious to know what 112 miles felt like (the distance cycled during an Ironman Triathlon), and I figured because this national event was held in my hometown, joining in would be the way to go.

Maggie and Payton dropped me off at *Thornapple Kellogg* (Middleville) *Middle School* around 7:40 a.m. for the 8:00 a.m. start. I think this is the least amount of prep time I have allowed before an event. I figured I would be warming up, doing the event, and cooling down, all throughout the course of this adventure. I positioned myself among over 500 riders near the rear. I have no regrets because I had a great view of the wheeled mass of humanity snaking along the curvy service road leading us to the first real road we traversed. It looked like something out of the *Tour De' France* with all the bright colored jerseys and helmets and the flow of the peloton making its way forward. It gave me chills. Oh wait…It was about fifty-seven degrees out, so the chills might have been from the air and the wind I was generating.

After the route took us out a few miles, we came back through downtown Middleville, where Maggie and Payton were waiting. All systems were go. I simply followed the lead of my fellow cyclists. We traveled quite slowly, relative to what I am used to during a training ride or triathlon. I was moving along at about fifteen mph, which is quite different from 20–23 mph, but when in Rome…

Because of wonder of whether or not my body would hold up during such a long ride, I planned various ways to return home or get to Hastings (Mom & Dad's). I figured if at the first checkpoint (34 miles) I was not feeling well I could turn around and come home. Sure it would be a 68 mile ride, but that is still a lot less than 126. On the way to the first checkpoint I moved from one small pack of riders to the next. The whole drafting thing made things a bit easier. I coasted down any and all hills I encountered, and I never put the chain in the big ring. I left my bike's computer in "distance" mode so I could see how I was feeling at various distances. Furthermore, I put black tape over the "speed" part of my computer so I would not be concerned with current pace. I needed to go by feel, and my mantra for the day was "*There is no such thing as too conservative.*" I practiced my mantra and arrived at the first checkpoint feeling fresh and ready to ease on down the road. I felt obligated to get off my bike at the checkpoint because it seemed like everyone else was. So, I got off and did a few stretches, then got back on my bike to continue my journey.

The terrain around Barry County offered rolling hills, flats, and some major hills. The variety was refreshing because all flats would have made me insane, and all hills would have kicked my butt; so the mix was perfect.

The second checkpoint was at mile 71, which was located at a church in the southeastern corner of Barry County. Arriving here was significant because this meant I was over half-way done, and I told myself if I got this far there was no going home or going to Hastings; there was just going forward. A very pleasant surprise occurred here because right after the officials verified my arrival, I saw two welcomed and familiar faces. My mom and dad had come to see how I was doing and to lend moral support! I thought that was great, but greetings were brief as the first order of business was to find the bathroom. Consuming lots of *Gatorade* can force these things you know. My folks didn't have to wait long for me to arrive because I had hit both checkpoints in the times I predicted. As a result, they knew when to arrive. They agreed to meet me at the next checkpoint (the 96 mile point), in order to continue providing encouragement, or to scoop me up off the pavement with a shovel and take me home.

More of the same types of terrain lead me to the third checkpoint. I continued the pace in which I began, and with the strategy which had been working well for me, and I made it to Delton at 2:00 p.m. as I had estimated. My folks were waiting for me with smiles on their faces and willingness to do what needed to be done. Dad filled my water bottle with water and Mom waited patiently while I again...hit the bathrooms. After discovering I was fairing well and was looking forward to going again, we went our separate ways. I began my final segment of the event, and Mom and Dad went home after visiting Tim and Jen's (Shaw) new baby Emilia.

On a single day's ride, I had only gone as far as 75 miles cycling my life, so I was particularly thrilled when my bicycle computer read "100.00" miles. "How cool is that?" I thought. Yeah, I know there are people who do this all the time, but not me. So what the hell; I had a big grin on my grill. I knew I only had twelve miles before I would know what my "Ironman split" would be. When "112.00" arrived I hit the button on my computer to see what it had to say, and my time was 7:07-something. This does include time at the checkpoints, but it was interesting for me to know. What does this mean for an Ironman? I don't exactly know what this means, but there it was.

I was in very familiar territory while I cruised along *Yankee Springs Road* and heading to the middle school. Not too dissimilar to a horse, I could tell my speed was steadily increasing because I knew I was getting closer to the proverbial "barn." I felt like I should tell the people I was passing to ignore me because I was a "One Loop Wonder". However, I decided it wasn't necessary, though I felt badly about passing them knowing they might be out on the course another several hours after I went home.

At last, I pulled into the middle school where it all began upwards of 126 miles earlier. I arrived with a sense of satisfaction, with a sense of accomplishment, and with a sense that there was a huge blister on my ass. Actually my rump held in there just fine. When I informed the director I was going home he responded inquisitively, yet encouragingly saying, "Really? You are? If you keep going you can get your 200 mile pin." After I briefly explained to him that I was happy my body held up this long, and that I still had to ride home he said, "Oh, you're from around here then? Are you the teacher here in town?" I confirmed his suspicion, we chatted a moment longer before I turned in my number and headed for home.

In the last three tenths of a mile of my ride home, I had a sinking feeling things were about to go south. Maggie was gone with the youngsters at a family function, and it dawned on me the house would be locked. "Sh#%!" was my thought, and the thought might have made it out of my mouth in the form of a shout, but fortunately the neighbor kids were not out playing. I imagined having to go to the neighbors asking for a peanut butter and jelly sandwich. This was of course because I was starving after having ridden my bike for 8+ hours. Luckily, Maggie had forethought enough to leave the door open for me, and I enjoyed my own PB & J's in the comfort of my own dining room…three of them actually.

My day ended with 130 miles of cycling. I think that's pretty cool. (I averaged 15.8 mph for the day).

## Clark Lake Triathlon, July 2004
## (.5mi/13mi/4mi)

"Five, Four, Three, Two, One, Go!" The race director shouted from the pier, as the men aged 20–34 stood anxiously up to their waists in water at the start. I discovered early that I positioned myself poorly. I found myself behind several rather large men who were not in as big of a hurry as I was and they enjoyed staying close to one another. This made getting around them quite challenging. Within 100 meters I received a large drink that I did not order, and was not expecting. Fortunately, I could stand in the water with my head out to cough, spit, and sputter while I gained my composure enough to empty out some of the unwanted beverage. Needless to say, I didn't leave a tip. After a few moments, I became poised once more, got going again, and found my rhythm. I was passing people and feeling good about my progress. Well, that is until I rounded the eastern-most buoy, sent us back toward the start. As I was rounding the buoy, another athlete was rounding his roundhouse and I got popped in the head and face. The force knocked my goggles up to my forehead and by reflex I let out an expletive. The guy was quick to apologize and I was equally quick to let him know it was ok, understanding it can be part of the business. I swam on my back as I adjusted my goggles before getting into the mix again. By the time I reached the shore I managed to put myself in mid-pack (twelfth in the 30–34).

*T1*: The *Clark Lake Triathlon* has a fairly long swim/run transition, but I didn't waste much time getting to it, and on my bike. However, I discovered I may need to apply more *Body Glide* to my ankles in the future, because my wetsuit was hanging on…again.

*The Bike*:The beginning of the bike course has athletes charging up a fairly steep hill, considering you are starting from zero anyway. In my mind, this was not a time to complain, but it was an opportunity to overtake some people. I passed several people going up the hill, and then I was rollin' wit' it. After the hill, the passing of people didn't stop. I felt strong and confident as I hammered my way down the road. I kept telling myself, "It's only 13 miles," or "It's only 10 miles," and so forth, depending on where I was on the course. Passing, instead of being passed is a very gratifying feeling. I have been on the receiving end of having a lot of people pass me in the past and it's a rush to be able to return the favor. The best people to pass are those I call "The big calf guys." As I go by I say in my head, "You're gonna' let this skinny guy pass you?" I have to believe they are wondering how I'm getting it done. The irony I suppose is that while I'm cycling, I envision myself as powerful and strong, and seemingly having calves and quads that are massive and relentless. I used a similar trick when I played football. Most people don't know that when I played little league football, I was 6'4" tall and 250 pounds…in my mind. Anyway, within the last 200 meters of the bike I had a Homer Simpson moment, because a guy passed me as we approached T2…*Doh!*

*T2*: With my bike racked, helmet off, running shoes and hat on, and race belt in hand, I was headed out.

*The Run*: I started the run conservative but steady. I finally found my rhythm around a mile into the race, and my mantra was "*You* can hold this for three miles," then "*You* can hold this for two miles," and so on. Though I increased my effort in the last 500–600 meters, I basically held my pace throughout the run. I crossed the line happy with how I performed and was pleased to be greeted by Maggie, Alex, Claudia, and Payton, and my friend Pete (Bodary) and his daughters Andi, Dana, and Caroline. I couldn't have asked for more.

# Spirit of Racine ½ Ironman, July 2004
## (1.2 mi/56mi/13.1mi)

Having the ability to simply participate in an event such as a half-Ironman is enough to feel grateful, and I am, but there is a selfish part of me that wants more. I went into the *Spirit of Racine ½ Ironman* with the understanding that I might have to drop out of the run early due to injuries I accumulated, and because of lack of better preparation as a result. However, whenever I toe the line of a half-Ironman, I can't help but to think about having a sub five-hour effort.

Going into Racine I knew five hours and thirty-minutes would be a more reasonable goal, and that I should feel good about achieving this goal if I reach it. I also knew that coming up with a 5:15-ish result was also possible with good fortune. Certainly producing a sub-five hour outcome, albeit requiring none other than a miracle would be outstanding, and of course the idea lingered half-heartedly in the back of my mind.

*The Swim*: The swim took place in the cool, but pleasant water of Lake Michigan, which displayed 2–3 foot swells. This was quite different from Bassett Lake where I train, where at times it may have one or two *inch ripples* from the wind. I knew my biggest challenge in the swim would be getting to the first buoy, because the waves were still breaking and crashing down until just before the first buoy. After the starting horn sounded, I ran with the rest of the 29–34 aged men into the crashing waves making my way by foot until the water was up to my chest.

Minutes before my start, I saw the pro men and then the pro women start their race day. They swam through the waves taking them head on, and seemingly without noticing the waves they encountered. They made it look easy so, I thought I would give it a go. Ok…they made it *look* easy. It wasn't. I found myself swimming on my back to get air as I floated up and over the waves. Since I was basically keeping pace with my bold counterparts around me who were doing the crawl (face down…normal), I continued to swim on my back while occasionally trying to swim the crawl myself. After utilizing the combination of swimming styles, I finally reached the first buoy and was able to swim parallel to the shore. While the rolling waves carried me up and down throughout the rest of the swim, I was able to swim with good rhythm and I felt strong and confident. It was very foreign to me swimming in such water, but it was great fun as well. One moment I would be at the top of a wave looking out at the next buoy and my competitors ahead of me. The next moment I was in a valley looking up, only seeing water around me. In due course, I made my way to shore and was greeted by the friends and families of the 1,500 participants who chose to discover the *Spirit of Racine*; my family included.

*T1*: To get to the first transition, we had to run 200 meters of sandy beach to the staging area. Once in transition things went smoothly, but it took me a little bit longer than a shorter distance triathlon, because there were other things to consider. I had to pack my *Cliff Bars* in the back of my jersey for example.

*The Bike*: The bike course began with a relatively long hill that got steeper as it went up, but the adrenaline rush carried me right up the hill and out to the streets of Racine. I found a steady cadence and passed quite a few people early. The hills of the bike course began showing themselves while we were still in the city, and they did not subside throughout the event. At no point did I look ahead of me and see a massive hill (ala Eastern Avenue Hills, for those of you who know the reference), but it seemed as though the whole time I was riding, I was either working up a long hill or recovering from one as I stared at the next. Another factor which made the course challenging was the wind. It was not especially windy, but it was windy enough that you could feel your energy being siphoned.

Nearing the halfway point of the ride, I was becoming more tired than expected for how early it was in the race. I had consumed one of my *Cliff Bars* by twenty-five miles and took some *GU*, and was regularly taking in *Gatorade*, but I was beginning to feel the effects of the wind and the hills. I determined if I had taken it out too fast in the beginning and was hoping the toll would not be too high. Around forty-five miles I became increasingly fatigued. I started to count down the miles, and when you start the countdown, it usually means you are anxious to get back. If you are anxious to get back, instead of anxious to kick butt, it's a pretty good sign you are about to get *your* butt kicked. Sure enough, cyclists began passing me instead of me passing them. I was hangin' in there, but I didn't want to hang in there, I wanted to take names. Approaching fifty-six miles I was happy to be on the city streets of Racine, and heading for the transition. However, I arrived spent, and after dismounting my *Litespeed*, I still had 13.1 miles to run.

*T1 & The Run*: Again my transition was slow, but after my shoes were tied and my hat was on, I grabbed my race-number-belt and headed for the exit. I took off like I was ready as ever to run a half-marathon, and the illusion even had *me* believing. Again exiting the transition, I faced the same long and steep hill I had taken on with my bike. Halfway up the hill I heard encouraging words from my brother Joe, and at this point I was feeling pretty good again.

The plan was to walk briefly at every aid station in order to consume enough water and *Infinite* (the sports drink they were offering). This was working for the first four or five miles, and things were going pretty well. My body however was beginning to feel the effects of my lack of better preparation. I began to really have doubts. The course was a double out and back and I was almost to the finish line. However, I had to turn around and go out again before I could come back (yes in some ways this was cruel). I imagined myself getting to the turn-around point, sitting down on the curb, and eating a big arse *Hoagie* and a bag of chips, while I watched the rest of the race go by. It sounded inviting but, I couldn't bring myself to drop out when I was healthy enough to finish; despite the fact that I was tired as heck. I grabbed some pretzels from the aid station table and another cup of *Infinite,* and started chewing on the dry, crunchy, salt-glazed stick, which was challenging to do with my dry mouth. I had decided, in spite of my vision of a curb-side picnicking, that I would not stop and drop out of the race. One thing that kept me going was something I read in *Triathlete Magazine* this summer. Ironman World Champion, Thomas Hellriegal had said something to this effect, "When things are going badly and you keep going you will forget the day, but if you drop out you will think about it all year." I didn't need *that* cloud hanging over me. A bigger thing keeping me going was Ang, Jay, and their family (Hoisington), Brian, Greta, and their family (Standish), Maggie and our kids, and Joe were all there to support me, and I wanted to at least finish the event they all drove so far, and got up so early for. I kept going.

My calves kept getting tight, my strength was leaving me, and my will was breaking, so my walking became more frequent. The goal of running to each mile marker became getting to that corner, and getting to a particular road sign, and so forth. It wasn't the first time I was in this kind of situation, but that didn't make it any less humbling. After the last aid station, which was near mile twelve, I told myself to just bring it in. Run the last mile! Go the distance! Make it happen! I started up again inspired to do good things!...400 meters later I was walking again. I didn't walk long though, because in the distance ahead of me I could hear the sound of the crowd, the music playing, the announcer letting the audience know who was finishing in front of me, and I knew I could make it. What I was doing at this point was arguably running, but I was putting one foot in front of the other, and I was determined to keep going until I crossed the finish line.

The last sixty meters or so was a long downhill which allowed me to let my legs go a bit, and I crossed the finish line. I shook a guy's hand and he said, "Congratulations." I accepted the finisher's medal from the girl who was handing them out, and then a water bottle from the next person. I put the medal around my neck so I wouldn't have to carry it. I began drinking the water while making my way toward the folding chairs set up for the participants to land on. Pretty soon I looked over and saw my supporters standing by the fence which was keeping the spectators away from the finisher's corral, and I walked over to give fives to those I could reach, and to give thanks to everyone for coming.

As I was gathering my gear, I was feeling dizzy and wasn't sure if I was going to pass out or throw-up. I managed to get my gear around, gave some to Joe, and met him outside the transition area where I gave him my bike and the rest of my stuff. I sat on the curb with my head between my knees waiting for the world around me to stop spinning. Over time I got in line for food, though I stood in line the whole time with my hands on my knees. I finally got some light food items and had a seat in the tent. Ang and Jay came to tell me they were leaving, but I didn't have the energy or willingness to stand-up. I figured they would rather not catch me, and they likely wanted to leave with clean shoes, so I stayed put. Thankfully Maggie and Joe took the kids and my gear, and brought the van around to get me. Later I recovered at Brian and Greta's where Brian fired up burgers on the grill.

It was a great trip and a wonderful adventure. I am grateful for all of the support I received and for the ability to participate in such an event. It was a challenge I enjoyed, on a journey that I know is not over.

## Mark Mellon Triathlon, August 2004
## (50 yd/1 mi/.75 mi)
### *Triathlete at Five*

It was not the first time she had been to a triathlon, because she had attended many, but the *Gaylord Kids Triathlon* would be different because instead of her doing the cheering, she would be doing the event. Alex decided she would enter the fifty yard swim, one mile bike, and ¾ mile run to get her feet wet in the sport of triathlon. This is only after being off training wheels for about two and a half weeks, not to mention still being afraid to go underwater while swimming.

At registration she was thrilled to receive her commemorative t-shirt and her race bag, which included her race numbers (201), course map, and white swim cap. She was officially registered. Alex soon consumed the spaghetti being offered to race participants and their families the evening before the event while at registration. She ate like a pro.

After a fairly rough night sleeping in the tent at Otsego Lake County Park where the event took place, Alex was asking if she should get ready for her race. Since it was only 7:00 a.m. and her race was not until 3:00 p.m. she settled for riding her bike around the campground loop yet again.

Her afternoon nap after lunch was not a total wash, because Alex did lie down for a while, but there would be no sleeping this time, and the preparations were beginning. Maggie dressed Alex in her bathing suit and shorts which were getting a number pinned to them and I affixed her other race number to her bicycle. Race time was about forty-five minutes away, and it was time to go set-up her transition area. She rode her bike behind Uncle Tim (Shaw), who was towing Claudia and Ada in the bike trailer, and Ali and Anisa rode their bikes along as well. Once in transition, Maggie assisted Alex in parking her bike, and placing her helmet and shoes in such a way that she would know where to get them once out of the swim.

With her cap on her head and a nervous grin on her face, she went to get body marked. The volunteers wrote her number on both arms and continued with the black marker, writing her age on her right calf. It was unusual for me seeing a single digit indicating ones age on the back of a triathlete's leg, but there it was. The only thing left to do before heading for the waterfront was put her "security" swimmies on her arms.

*The Swim*: Along with other triathletes aged five through eight, Alex stood in the water just above her waist while listening to the final instructions given by the race director. Finally, with the path cleared, the starter's pistol was fired, and the race began. One or two of the athletes actually swam, while the rest of the kids charged through the water running as fast as they could in the resisting water. "There she is!" We shouted from shore when we saw her. She was bouncing up and down happily alongside some of the others who shared last place with her. The yellow and blue swimmies helped distinguish her from the other small triathletes who were all sporting white caps.

*T1*: The swim-to-bike transition involved running from the beach to the transition area, which was about 100 yards away. Across the sand, up the stairs, and along the carpet laid for tender feet, she ran. Once her cap and swimmies were off and her helmet and shoes were on, she mounted her bike and put rubber to the road, with many in front of her, and several behind.

*The Bike*: When cycling there are many factors in finding success, and one of the biggest is *not* having a mechanical failure. While rounding the first corner, Alex's bike hit a bump causing her loose-fitting chain to fall off. Her legs were spinning rapidly as her bike floated along the campground road, and she was losing many positions in the race. I happened to be at the corner, so I ran over to her to assist the best I could. She was beginning to cry. She wasn't crying because there was a real possibility she would finish dead last, but rather, as she said it better than I can, "Now there are no kids for me to follow." After the bike was flipped over, I struggled to get the chain on and I was failing miserably. This in part was due to freaking out and in part to not having very good positioning with Payton on my back in the backpack. Maggie ran over and put the chain on in short order. We were encouraging Alex to go on, but she was already riding…She was back in the race!

The bikes were cruising the campground very quickly with excited young triathletes, and though Alex was buzzing along holding the last position, she had a smile on her face. It was obvious she was enjoying herself with friends and family at nearly every part of the course yelling encouraging words and cheering for her.

*T2*: As she attempted to enter the transition area, Alex encountered a wall of over zealous parents helping all of the kids who had come in before her, and she was unable to access her transition area. Hmm, no wonder in adult triathlons only athletes are allowed in the transition area. Eventually she made her way through the crowd of towering people and the confusion. It was our intention that Alex would perform her transition tasks herself, but with the assistance of an uninvited, unknown adult, she removed her helmet, racked her bike, and was on her way.

*The Run*: Recognizing Alex might be feeling a bit disoriented from the confusion of the transition, with people going every which way shouting numerous instructions, Maggie ran along Alex's side until she was able to get her bearings on the run. Before the race, and after again hearing the "You are out there just for fun" speech from Maggie, Alex said, "I *at least* want to have *one* person behind me." Well, in the not-so-far-off distance there was a young girl who was walking, and Maggie asked Alex, "Do you remember when you told me you wanted at least *one* person behind you?" She responded with the kind of "yeah" which begged the question, "What are you about to tell me here?" Maggie continued, "Well," pointing ahead to the girl, "there she is." With that Alex picked up her pace with only another turn to go before the straightaway, which led to the finish line. Running as smoothly as a five-year-old can, she sailed past the girl, rounded the curve, gave it what she had and as she finished to the sound of cheering from her friends, family, and all those who were lining the course to the finish. With a wide smile on her face and an evident sense of accomplishment, she finished her first triathlon not last, but with one person behind her.

Alex not only went home with a finisher's medal, a t-shirt, and a white swim cap, she walked away with a positive experience in her first triathlon.

Additional notes: *Alex finished second in the 5–6 year-old division. My niece Anisa won the 9–10 year-old division. My nephew Ali was third in the 11–12 year-old division. Each division had its own race with different race distances. Oh, and I won the Short Course Triathlon.*

## Three Rivers Triathlon (Short Course), August 2004 (300m/18km/5km)

Some might say me racing in the short course events is like snuffing my little sister while playing basketball, which isn't as easy as it sounds, because not everyone has talented basketball players for sisters like I do. However, others may argue it is simply a preference of distance in which to compete. I hope to write to *Triathlete Magazine* about this issue to gain clarity, but for now let me get on with it.

If you have ever woken up in the morning, on a fine summer day, to be welcomed by a temperature to the tune of 53-degrees and thought to yourself, "Dude, I have *GOT* to go swimming!" Then you probably won't have much sympathy regarding the start of the *Three Rivers Triathlon*. I stood on the shore with my arms wrapped around my shivering body waiting for my wave to be called, so I could enter the cool waters of *Corey Lake* for the first leg of my event.

*The Swim*: Once in the water with my fellow competitors, I was pumped and ready to go. Looking around I knew it would be no cakewalk, but I was still priming myself for a top three finish. After the starting horn sounded, we were off and thrashing in the water toward the outer-most orange buoy which was all of 150 meters from the start. Although it was not a long swim, I chose to wear my wetsuit. Call it my comfort, call it being a wimp, call it warmth for most of my body while waiting for the start, but I'm calling it good, because I hung in there with the lead pack. I exited the swim in around fourth place. I had a plan of gaining some ground in transition, which was quite a long trip from the water. I took my wetsuit off about fifteen yards on land, so I could run with it to my rack. This tactic allowed me to pass a couple people before I reached my bike and gear.

*T1*: With my wetsuit already off, and tossed in a heap out of the way, I strapped my shoes on, buckled my helmet, adjusted my glasses, pulled my bike from the rack, and started jogging to the bike exit.

*The Bike*: Once mounted on my *Litespeed,* all I was thinking about was crankin' out of the main entrance and droppin' the hammer. I knew it was a hilly course, but I also recognized I needed to quickly get up where the action was and make a race of it. I passed one person right away, and then I didn't see anyone for a while, as I ascended and descended the hills, and went screaming around the many curves on the road. "Keep pushing," I told myself, "They're up there somewhere." I shouted to a volunteer, "How many ahead?" I heard, "Uhn". Ok, is that one, none? I don't know how to talk? "C'mon, just go!" I told myself, though I was beginning to feel the effects of the hill I was climbing.

When I saw the competition in the distance, my adrenaline gave me another boost, my pace quickened, and I was pumped, because I knew I was going to reel him in. As the halfway point in the course disappeared behind us, I knew if I was going to put some time in between he and I before the run, I had to make a move here. It took longer than I hoped, but I finally came up on him after a downhill, and at the same time about to go up *another* hill. I gave a little more than I felt I had, and I put in a pass I hoped would lead him to believe he had no chance of hanging onto my wheel. I flew up the first three-quarters of the hill and could feel it pulling on me like an anchor, and my hope was that my pursuer wouldn't see my struggle. After I crested the hill, I was finally relieved to be going downhill again. Relaxing was not an option however, so even though my legs were grateful for the short-lived relief, I went to a bigger gear and pushed the pace.

At this point, the goal was to maximize my advantage because I didn't know what I had in me for the run. My leg had been bothering me more since the *Mark Mellon* event, so I wasn't sure if it would continue to trouble me. I put my head down and tried to let the field pay their own dues. I didn't look back and just had to believe there was no response from my adversary.

*T2 & Run*: My cycling shoes decided today was the day to let me know the *Velcro* straps were working just fine, thank you very much. The experience was similar to attempting to blow out trick birthday candles. Each time I had the straps undone, they went right back into place. This exercise in persistence only lasted a moment, but it was enough to fluster me into believing I was losing any advantage I earned on the bike, to an athlete on my heels who was an expert at bike-to-run transitions. Of course I didn't really know. For all I knew, he transitioned slower than anyone else that day, but in the heat of the moment, that wasn't my vision. Nevertheless, I got out and was moving along, curious about what my body would allow today.

Within the first half-mile I asked a group of volunteers, "Any ahead?" This time I received a very clear response, but it wasn't the one I was pulling for. "Just one!" Of course I assumed it was the guy I passed on the bike, with my imagined pro-like transition skills, and also I figured he couldn't be too far ahead of me. Three-quarters-of-a-mile into the run I saw the guy who was between me and winning the race. I was surprised to see it wasn't who I thought it was. Somebody I never saw on the bike course beat me back on the bike and was still leading.

I had gradually gained on the leader and was within 100 meters going up the hill to the turn-around (half-way point). Knowing he would see me on his way back, I pushed myself up the hill to gain as much ground as I could. Normally I would give some words of encouragement to my fellow competitors, but not today. I was the hunter, he was the hunted, and this lion was hungry for that gazelle.

Going down the hill after the turn-around, I reduced the real estate between us and I gained confidence. I spotted "Mr. Speedy Transition" charging around the corner to go up the hill to the turn-around where I had just been, and I knew at that moment that I couldn't just go after the leader. I also needed to battle the hunter behind me. Apparently hungry lions were not lonely today.

Approaching the two-mile marker, I passed the leader and put in a surge going up the long hill we were on, and didn't let up until I was going down the other side.

"How far back?" I asked athletes headed out on their first half of the course…nothing. I kept asking different athletes, and still nothing. After seeing the final hill leading into the staging area, I asked again and this time a volunteer said, "You've got a ways." I wasn't sure what his "ways" was compared to my "ways" and I wanted this win, so I continued on steadily, concerned enough not to let up.

Once inside the staging area, I had 200 meters to go, and I covered it without being passed, and to the sounds my family shouting, "Go daddy!" I did it…I won!

The next competitor, who also passed the original leader, came through about 30–40 seconds later. As it turned out he ran faster than I did, so the effort on the bike paid off. Oh yeah!

# Chapter Six: Race Fans 2005

## 2005 Pre-season Thoughts

As I stand before the threshold of my tenth season in triathlon, I am facing an all-too-familiar scenario…beginning the season injured. I have been addressing my problems and have experienced gains, but not as quickly as I would like. Furthermore, an additional problem has come up. Through research via Internet and consultations with my physical therapist Scott (Miller), we have concluded that I have some muscle imbalances to address, and weak gluteus muscles to strengthen. I have been working for some time with physical therapy exercises, have been professionally fit to both of my bicycles to maximize efficiency, and I believe my IT Band issues are becoming less prevalent. However, within the past month I have developed a problem in my right knee which I believe is strained tendons. This is particularly disappointing because my knee becomes irritated when I cycle, and this activity has been my saving grace since being unable to run. I have been making gains with my cycling and am hoping this will be my strength this season, so it is discouraging to have a problem in this area. I am however, still attempting to carry an optimistic point of view.

Today is June 5th and on June 18th my first major event of the season will take place in the form of the *National 24-Hour Challenge*. This of course is a bicycling event. Last year I completed the first loop of 126 miles and this year I hope to go 200 miles. However, health, good weather, and good fortune will be strong determinants in my success. I am nervous and disheartened as I type this, because it is my second day of *complete* inactivity, and there is ice on my knee doing its work to help heal my wounded knee.

My running is to the point where I can run very slowly for three miles pain free, and this is encouraging, but again, my knee has put a temporary halt on this activity as well. If my running continues to improve I will consider doing *United States Triathlon Association* (USTA) sanctioned events, and *Michigan Grand Prix Series* (MGPS) events to seek points in each, and try to put together a strong season. However, if my running does not allow me to go at least six-to-seven miles at a strong clip, I will defer to short course events which do not accumulate points in either of the aforementioned areas.

Today is especially difficult because I want to get out and cycle and run, but I am doing everything I can to keep myself sedentary and keep to a regular icing schedule. I do have a saving grace in swimming. Swimming is something I am able to do and I have been fairly consistent with my twice—a-week regiment. I have come to the conclusion however, that I am not getting faster in this area due to my stubbornness to take the time to learn all of the precise skills necessary to up the ante. So, I am maintaining my swimming ability which is respectable, but not spectacular.

At present I have a few different schedule scenarios depending on what my body will allow me to do. Time will tell what direction I will be able to go. I want to move ahead at full throttle, but I know the best course of action is to be patient, and I will try to be.

## National 24-Hour Challenge, June 2005 (As Far As You Can Ride In 24-Hours)

When you look at the number 200 you see it is very clean and neat, and when it comes to cycling, saying you cycled 200 miles sounds pretty darn good. Last year for the *24-Hour Challenge*, I managed to cover the first loop of 126 miles and was quite pleased with the effort, but approaching this year's event I was looking for more. This year I thought 200 miles would be the magic number. Two-hundred is fun to look at and fun to say, unless of course you are referring to how much you owe, or how many gallons of ice cream you think you consumed over the course of the summer. Again, on paper it looks good, and it rolls off the tongue handsomely, but after covering the first 126 mile loop I didn't much care about the beauty of the number 200 any more.

The morning greeted us with temps in the mid-fifties and cloudy skies. The start of this event is my favorite part to view because the rolling mass of humanity is an incredible sight to see. We followed the curves of the service road behind the *Thornapple Kellogg Middle School* and began heading southbound on Bender Road. Here we were all traveling together for the moment, with expectations ranging from covering the most miles of anyone else in 24-hours, to making it to the first check-point of the first loop. We were young and old, fat and skinny, brightly colored in technical apparel, and loosely fit in cut-offs and t-shirts. We all had our own goals, and though some of us were competing against each other, most of us were competing against ourselves and happened to share the same asphalt.

The temperature slowly increased, but the clouds remained, and so the weather was comfortable and welcoming. We faced rolling hills, steep inclines, rapid descents, pancake flat stretches, winding roads, and the diversity kept us alert and challenged throughout the first loop. There wasn't anywhere else I wanted to be, and I was grinning, mostly without realizing it, until around 88 miles. At this point my journey alternated between joy and pain. I went back and forth between thinking I was having a lot of fun, to thinking of ways to get my drained body to the next check-point. Certain things would spark energy into me and I would be good for several miles. For example, it was great seeing "100.00" on my cyclocomputer, which let me know I had covered 100 miles. It was thrilling going down an exceptionally long and steep hill at about 40 mph, and it was inspiring when I finally reached the roads I train on regularly when I got closer to the end of loop one. However, at about 118 miles it was a struggle. My *Gatorade* was gone, I was sick of eating *Cliff Bars*, though I forced my fourth one down anyway, and my neck and upper-back were tight as a drum. I finally rolled in the final check-point of loop one, and I knew the magic number 200 was not going to happen today.

After sitting with Maggie, Payton, and my mom and dad, I got hydrated again with the assistance of *Gatorade* and water. I got to my feet and headed for the door with encouragement and with the benefit of a neck and back massage from Mom. Although I had decided I was not going to go for 200 miles, I was determined to complete the 23 mile second loop. As I rolled along at a manageable pace, I began to feel more energized, but this was not enough to persuade me to go another loop. Upon completion of my final loop and covering 150 miles, I was greeted by Maggie, Alex, Claudia, and Payton, and I got hugs from them all. I checked in my score card and number, loaded my bike and worn-out carcass into the van, and we drove off, while others lingered on long into the night and into the early morning hours chasing their own personal magic numbers.

Throughout this year's event I wore on my right wrist my yellow Lance Armstrong *"LIVE STRONG"* bracelet and on it in black ink, the names *Joe Kasper* and *Anne Lillie*. Please keep them in your prayers while both of them battle their respective cancers.

## Waterloo Triathlon, July 2005
## (.5 mi/16mi/5mi)

After the drama of getting Claudia and Payton out of bed at 3:55 a.m., and settling them into car seats to watch *The Letter Factory*, our in-van movie, we were on our way to the *Waterloo Recreation Area*, just north of Jackson, Michigan. Alex was still sleeping at her Grandma Haraburda's house when the race began at 8:00 a.m., so she missed the action.

*The Swim*: Though this particular event has been around for many years, this was my first go of it, and though I was familiar with the general area, I didn't know what this course had to offer. The swim was deemed a non-wetsuit affair when the officials announced the water temperature was 79 degrees (78 degrees and lower is legal wetsuit temperature). I was comfortable with this because I had been doing half of my workouts without a wetsuit in anticipation of this scenario. Air temps had been in the low-to-mid 90's for much of June, but having a wetsuit is still a security that would have been enjoyed.

After a minor delay, the horn blasted and the male's age groups of 30–34 and 35–39 were underway. Our green-swim-capped heads bobbed in the water while our arms and legs generated enough splashing to provide the illusion that a strange species of fish had schooled up and were headed out for deeper water. It's always great to begin the swim feeling strong and confident, and I was feeling both. I had an inside "lane" and was in a steady rhythm. People were getting passed and I was sighting dead on to the next giant, oversized, orange marshmallow-looking buoy. Things were good…until they weren't.

At most modern functioning triathlons, athletes are given a neoprene strap which goes around one's ankle. The strap has a computer chip attached to it for timing purposes. It's a great thing because results and race splits are available in very short order. The race officials remind you however, that should the chip be lost during the course of the event, the loser of the strap and chip will pay $30.00 to replace it. After passing the second of six buoys I could feel the strap on my pencil-thin ankle begin to slide down toward my foot. This was very distracting. Remember the $30.00? Yeah, well me too. I continued to swim normally hoping the strap would just settle into a lower position on my leg…no such luck. It continued to snail its way further south. I pulled over to the side to avoid traffic, dunked my head toward my foot, while pulling my knee toward my body; similar to doing a jack-knife underwater. From the lifeguard's perspective, it probably looked as though I had given up, rolled myself up into a ball and wished to drift off so nobody would see me. I re-adjusted the strap so it was nice and snug and it was…at least for the moment. This happened a few more times before I finally reached the shore in a position further back than I should have been. However, I made it back to shore which is always the first goal when swimming. Trotting out of the water I was welcomed by the words I love to hear and surprisingly the most volume and enthusiasm came from Payton, as Maggie, Claudia, and Payton shouted, "Go daddy go! Go daddy go!"

*T1*: My goggles, cap, and earplugs were taken out on my way to transition, so they were easily discarded. I quickly wiped my feet, strapped on my brain bucket, etc. and for the last time during the event, I tightened the strap on my ankle.

*The Bike*: This was my time to make up for lost ground. I knew the bike would be my strongest leg of the event today and I wanted to make the best of it. I passed two athletes right away after I clipped in, and all they could do was listen to the sweet sound of my three-spoked, carbon fiber wheels buzzing by, while they attempted to put their shoes in their pedals. Two more victims were claimed before I exited the park to take on the local, hilly, and winding roads which circle the lake. I then found myself alone, but *far* from the lead. I kept a high cadence and had to really concentrate to keep pushing the pace because nobody was in sight. There was a race happening way in front of me somewhere, but I couldn't see it. I was being pursued, but I only had the knowledge not the evidence from being an eyewitness. I began to wonder if I should have taken a left back at Alba-coiky (ala *Bugs Bunny*). Finally, off in the distance I spotted my target and I was relieved to know I was still on the course. It took a little time, but I patiently over-took the rider while going up a hill. A strong move was a must to put in his brain the idea that he wasn't going to stay with me. Although it seemed like a long time, it was only a few moments before my next adversary was in view. Again I was patient on my approach, but then I dropped the hammer in order to buzz by in such a way that was a serious blow to his confidence. Then I wheeled on in search of the next. One or two more fell off the pace before I rolled into the transition area. I counted about eight runners who had finished the bike segment well before me, and later I learned at least two were far enough in front of the ones I saw, that I couldn't count them. This allowed reality to inform me I was doing well, but not to get too excited.

*T2*: It probably *looked* like I was going to trip and fall as I rushed by the racks of bikes while simultaneously pushing my bike, and hitting the "lap" button on my watch, but I was under control...really. After switching from brain bucket to head lid, and cycling shoes to running dogs, I was headed out.

*The Run*: To keep up with the theme I started in about 1994, I began the run thinking about an injury. Since my knee and hip injuries were mostly at bay, my left Achilles tendon (where it attaches to my calf) determined it was its turn to plague me. My goal for the run was to be able to run the entire way and not have to walk to the finish. I kept a deliberately slow and cautious pace through the first two miles. The crunching sound of the gravel under my feet on the dirt road, and the birds singing in the trees kept me company, because after a guy running like a bat out of hell passed me just before mile one, I was alone again.

The dirt roads were filled with large rolling hills, which ultimately brought me to a trail which continued this trend but added its own many twists, turns, ruts, and the like. I looked over my shoulder every once in a while expecting to see somebody coming. "Let's go people! I'm going *slow* for crying out loud." I wasn't looking forward to being passed, but I assumed it would happen sooner or later considering my pace. Though I just wanted to get it over with, there were no takers. I kept my "jogging" pace while only occasionally feeling discomfort in my calf, which reminded me not to even think about trying to go faster, and still nobody passed me. Exiting the woods I was expecting to be in a different part of the park than I was so, I had to reorient myself with the help of race volunteers in the course's last stretch. I heard Payton yelling in a commanding voice, "Go daddy! *Daddy, go!*" It was great to hear him, and it was inspiring not only because he is my two-year-old son watching me do what I love, but because he sounded genuinely concerned that I pick up the pace. He was shouting like a coach to his athlete. I coasted across the finish line, grabbed some water, and enjoyed the warm summer morning, and the joy of having completed another triathlon. Another great event had been completed, in the sport I love.

*The Incredibles* played on the DVD for sleeping children, and we cruised down I-94 on our way back to Middleville, where the rest of the day carried on.

## Interlochen Triathlon, July 2005
### 500m/20k/5k

At least once a season, taking in a large gulp of unexpected and unwanted water is in order, and today was my day. The water temperature in Duck Lake, at Interlochen State Park, just south of Traverse City was 80 degrees, so wetsuits were out. All of the males competing in the short course lined up and faced the first buoy which was less than fifty meters away. When the horn sounded the start of the race, the wide mouth of the funnel of swimmers became narrow in short order. In attempts to establish myself early and gain position, I sprinted out and reached oxygen debt early. My hope was to be one of the first to round the buoy and settle into my own pace thereafter. What happened instead was my heart rate accelerated and I met many others attempting the same feat as myself. The result was an unintended handful of water being delivered to my mouth for my efforts. Already being short of breath, the water added insult to injury, and I found myself doing the side stroke while sputtering like a tea kettle. Still not recovering fast enough to get back into the mix, I shifted to the backstroke. Finally, I got enough water out and enough air in, and I turned over to make an attempt at salvaging my swim. I arrived at shore giving the leaders a comfortable cushion with hopes that this was the last water intake I would receive during a swim this season.

*T1*: From the beach we ran up an embankment to the parking lot which served as the transition area. At least five or six athletes chose to jog very slowly, apparently taking in the scenery and the sounds of the encouraging fans. I took advantage of their generosity by running by them.

*The Bike*: There was a narrow tree-lined, paved path that led us to the road which provided an illusion of traveling fast through a spectator laden course. Once I hit the road I was on the hunt for as many athletes as I could find. After a lackluster swim, having a strong bike was imperative. I was focused and determined, and I passed many good swimmers along the way. As I was getting closer to the turn around point, I counted cyclists as they were on their return trip and five were in front of me at this point. I was feeling more confident about my leg's ability to carry me through the run with greater intensity than last week, but I didn't want to depend on it. My goal was to put some time in on the competition before T2, but the leaders were putting time in on me instead.

*T2*: Quick and to the point. I rushed out in pursuit.

*The Run*: I started out with a certain amount of caution, while paying attention to any signals my calf/Achilles might be sending, but additionally with the idea in mind that I was going to push the pace. After a short jaunt down a wooded path, I was greeted by the paved drive which went through the campground. My leg was holding up well and I had gone up a pretty good hill without signs of discomfort, so I gradually increased my pace. By the time I reached the turn-around, there were only a few in front of me. The first two looked smooth, and seemed to have a good rhythm; the third however was like the ill elk this wolf would commit to early. I rounded the orange cone marking our turn and focused on the elk in front of me. My pace continued to increase and I took the first of my targets. I saw my next target was quite a bit farther ahead, and that a guy in blue and orange was moving quickly with a fluid gait toward the turnaround. He too seemed to be thinking he would get a hold of the weakened elk before trying to take on the next wolf on his hunt, and thus become the alpha-male. I lost sight of my target, but pressed on knowing I was being rapidly pursued. After covering the rolling hills in the campground, I rounded the curve on the wooded trail taking me to the finish shoot which was lined with spectators. Before I entered the tunnel of people, I heard my supporters shouting encouragement, and I cruised across the remaining fifty meters, consequently crossing the finish line shortly thereafter.

As it turned out, one of the two men in front of me was participating in the duathlon that was going on in conjunction with my event, and this meant I earned second overall.

We spent another few days enjoying Traverse City with my sister Jen and her family before returning home. This included a bike ride I took up M-37 North to the lighthouse at its end. It's fair to say a good time was had by all.

## Great Lakes Triathlon, July 2005
## (.5mi/18mi/4.8mi)

It was great being able to sleep in until 5:45 a.m. on a triathlon morning, and having only to travel ten minutes to the race, which happens to be as near to my backyard as any triathlon around. Muggy conditions greeted us in the morning with temps in the mid-60s, and with the promise of temps reaching near 90 by day's end. The sun was making itself known, but the canopy of trees lining the *Barlow Lake YMCA* entrance and the transition area kept us cool. Friendly and familiar faces were all around getting their gear set-up in transition, and things were looking good.

To my pleasant surprise, I stood in the 80 degree, non-wetsuit permitted water, up to my knees with several former Caledonia alums who were giving triathlon a go. Chris VanRyn, Ryan Berends, and Kevin Tafelski were standing with me as we chatted only somewhat nervously before our wave's start. It was a thrill for me to have them there because it added a new dimension to my endeavor. A new challenge was now set before me. Were they better swimmers than I? Have they been logging more cycling miles than me? Would they outrun me? With all due respect, I didn't really think any of these things were happening or would happen today, but I didn't assume anything either. They were mostly there to have fun. I was mostly there to have fun *and* have a strong showing in front of the hometown crowd.

Unfortunately, Maggie and the kids were unable to attend today's event. Maggie was well into the first game of many she would play at the *Wayland Summerfest Softball Tournament* while the kids were in good hands at Jen and Tim's house. I wasn't however without hearing the words, *"Go daddy go!"* A young boy's voice shouted this out prior to the start and many of the men 34 and younger turned to see if it was from his own child. Only one man was able to legitimately make the claim, but many of us accepted the encouragement just the same.

*The Swim*: All systems were go and I was pleased with the effort, and the well executed plan of starting conservative, building speed, and joining the pack.

*T1*: Another uphill climb to a transition, and once more gracious triathletes taking their sweet time, offering me a chance to regain the positions I had lost to them on the swim. Thanks guys!

*The Bike*: With the woman's waves beginning ahead of us, there were a lot of people out on the bike course. Early on I received some energy inducing words from Josh (Reynolds) who happened to be volunteering at the accompanying duathlon (thanks Josh). Approaching about 1.5 miles my friend and co-worker Marc (Lester) gave a shout. I was feeling strong and enjoying passing people while remaining in pursuit of others still ahead of me. Around four and a half miles I was surprised to see Maggie. She had parked on a side road and was providing encouragement. I was feeling strong and was holding a high cadence as my bike propelled me down the smooth, rolling road. After the turn-around at Wayland High School, and getting just out of town, I ascended a long hill and felt better than expected, and so I really dropped the hammer at the crest. At nearly the close of a respectable ride, I brought it home and was ready to run.

*T2*: In...switch-a-roo...out.

*The Run*: There he was again giving out the love freely. Josh gave me a high-five about a half mile into the run (thanks *again* Josh)! I ran on with more confidence than concern, which was different from any of my previous events this year, and I held on to a respectable pace. No land speed records were in jeopardy, but it was a decent clip. I strode in only seconds behind a twenty-seven year-old I was chasing during the bike, but never caught. After giving up my timing chip to the volunteers, I took a quick rinse in the lake, gathered my gear, and rushed off to Jen's to relieve her and Tim of Wilkinson child watch duty.

It was a good day and a solid performance. I felt much better than I expected, and was glad I could get it together for the most local event I do. Oh! For those curious, the other former Caledonian's didn't catch me...today anyway.

## Cycling Adventures, July 2005
### It's not about the bike...but sometimes it is <u>AND</u> every second *does* count. (Rapid Wheelmen Ride and Ada Time Trial)

I didn't expect to be cruising along the roads leading to New Salem with Hodge (Tim Hodgkinson) and about 60 or so others, nor did I expect to ride a steady 45 miles instead of a moderate 38 miles, the day before the August 1st Ada Time Trial, but there I was. If it hadn't been for the *Rapid Wheelmen Newsletter*, I would not have known Hodge was back on his bike after a many-year hiatus. We e-mailed back and forth and came to the conclusion on Sunday morning that we would be meeting at the *Ramblewood Racquet Club* that afternoon to ride with the *Rapid Wheelmen* and two other clubs from the area. The ride started out relaxed and easy, given that Hodge and I held mid-pack amidst the sea of cyclists. Our peloton made its way to Byron Center and began heading westward on 84th Street. Hodge and I worked our way up in the group in order to remain in contact with the front pack because the groups of riders began to separate. The map we were given before the ride had both written directions and a photocopied map of the area. Recognizing the area and what I *thought* was the route; I neglected to pay close attention to the details. You know, like which way we were riding the figure eight course. Part of the course took us on Homerich, which I had ridden many times during my time living at Ramblewood Apartments, and while living in the house on 68th Street. In my mind, we were going to take Homerich south before heading west again in order to go beyond New Salem. Unfortunately, what was in my mind and what was written clearly on the map were distinctly different. However, I didn't reach this conclusion before explosively taking off toward the front of the pack where the heavy hitters were. It was my intention to let them know we had passed Homerich a couple roads back, and that we were off course. Once I was at the front (minus two guys who were neither interested in relinquishing their lead positions, nor in hearing the skinny guy tell them they were going the wrong way), I gave my "The sky is falling" speech and everyone in the lead positions started looking at one another clearly second guessing the course we were on. Finally, one of the guys with a bright-colored cycling jersey, which could have read, "I have giant calves and huge thighs and could eat you for lunch," grunted, "We're going to Eighth Avenue." I decided at this point, like I should have prior to racing to the front, that it didn't really matter because we would get there either route we took.

After turning on Eighth, Hodge and I got dropped by the lead pack with only the chance to look at each other wondering what just happened. So, we cruised along chatting about whatever, until we reached near the outermost point of the ride. We didn't realize it was time to start heading back because we turned left at the intersection and went on, opting not to stop for ice cream like the rest of the group. After another forced left, we followed a road for some time before heading back north toward our starting point. Our next mistake was taking a right when we should have gone straight. Ultimately we corrected ourselves and were back on the course and the lead group caught up to us. We decided our response, if they asked what happened to us was that we decided to take an alternate route…not that we screwed up a couple turns and covered almost ten extra miles. They were probably just proud they caught us so quickly, since they hung out and ate ice cream and we hadn't. We were about to reach the main drag bringing us back to our cars when I dropped my *PowerGel* packet on the ground. "I'll uh, catch up…or I won't, but I've dropped something!" I shouted to Hodge, who was just in front of me with the pack. He graciously turned around with me and we headed back, and once again we were by ourselves. I felt badly about losing the pack and I still thought we could catch them if we dropped the hammer for a half mile or so, and I said, "Grab on!" as I clenched the drop bars and took it to anther level. My hope was that Hodge was right behind me and we would soon catch the pack. I saw that we were making some small gains and I wasn't ready to give up, but then…a red light. We stopped after a 200 meter full-out attempt at catching up and conceded the fact that the pack was rolling in without us.

It was a great ride, great company, and a great course. We cruised into the parking lot feeling good and with our, "Yeah, we meant to do that" look on our faces, as we saw the others swigging down their energy drinks and talking about their cool bikes. Hodge and I disassembled our bikes enough to load them in our respective vehicles, shook hands, and were off.

I wish I could say this is the end of the story for our ride, but there's more. After exiting the parking lot I headed down the road taking me to 44th Street, which later took me to US-131 and so forth. Another pack of riders was across from me preparing to go straight at the light, and I had my blinker on because I was preparing to turn left. You ever catch yourself not thinking straight? This was one of those moments for me, which could have ended quite tragically. I'm sure you see the writing on the wall here. The light turned green and I started to go. I saw the cyclists were also going so I accelerated to get out of their way. I heard some grumblings, but no expletives like I deserved. For whatever reason, it didn't occur to me that they had the right of way, but very clearly they did. So, at my first official ride (outside of time trials) as a *Rapid Wheelmen*, I caused confusion about the direction we were going on the ride, took a wrong turn adding nearly ten miles to the ride, dropped my gel packet, thus losing the group, and just about took out a whole pack of riders on my way out. Is it so bad I had a great time anyway? Here's the thing; I just can't ever show up to any rides with my silver Ford Taurus anymore. Well, that is unless I have a sign reading, "Yes, I *am* the bastard who nearly killed you," and just come clean.

Yesterday, I went to Ada for my third time trial this year, ready to do battle with the regulars. This is a 15 mile event where riders are sent off every minute to see how fast one can cover the course. Drafting is not legal and basically *an*aerobic is the order of the day. Anyway, I wasn't sure how it would go having done the 45 mile ride the previous day, but I decided to give it a go. My previous best was 36:32, which was highly inspired due to ominous storm clouds and the knowledge that our kids were driving Maggie nuts back at the park where we start and finish. That's another story. Nevertheless, the starter counted down from ten. "Ten, nine, eight…one!" My first pedal stroke was strong and full of conviction, but to my dismay my next stoke was full of fumbling and slippage. My cleat did not click into my pedal and there I coasted for just a couple seconds, until I finally made the connection I needed. This was the moment that cost me. This was the moment I now look at, which prevented me from a P.R. (Personal

Record). I'm thrilled to tell you I was first out of the 29 riders who showed up for the time trial, and frankly delighted with my time, but at 36:33 I was only two seconds away from a new P.R. So, it *can* be about the bike, and every second *does* count when you are hoping to maximize your efforts.

## Mark Mellon Triathlon, August 2005
### *Long*: (1000m/50k/10k); *Short*: (200yd/12mi/3mi)

As we stumbled out of our respective tents and camper, we were greeted by a brisk fifty-two degrees, and though backs were stiff and sleep deprivation was in full swing, we began our preparations to compete at the 2005 *Mark Mellon Triathlon*. Tim and Jen brought with them an entire pit crew by way of all of their children and two of Anisa's friends, who attended a basketball camp earlier the same week. The Shaw family leaders, after a year break were committed to taking on the short course at *Mark Mellon* once again. After meandering around for about half an hour and starting my own preparations, I made my way to the Shaw camper to attempt to awaken the not-so-rested duo. Once the door was opened, a gentle reminder did the trick. "Let's go rookies!" With blurred vision and bed heads to boot, they stepped out into the chilly morning. "I feel like going for a swim," Jen retorted with evident sarcasm and her breath hanging in the air in a light fog.

The men competing in the short course event kicked things off. With a blast of the horn, the race commenced. As they headed toward the sun, all we could see was the silhouettes of various body types thrashing through water up to their waists before plunging in the cool waters of Otsego Lake, where the first leg of the triathlon began. Tim was among the mob and would soon make his way out of the water and head for his bike.

Jen and other the women of the short course triathlon started in similar fashion a few minutes after the men. Leading the charge was none other than Audrey Hoag, a former student of mine, former cross country and track athlete of Maggie's, and a friend of ours who comes from a family of triathletes. After her swim, Jen stormed out and chased the orange lines to transition.

*The Swim & T1*: The third wave consisted of the men competing in the long course triathlon which included yours truly. Learning from my *Great Lakes Triathlon* experience, I started on the outside and worked my way into the pack, after establishing a steady rhythm. Ultimately I managed a respectable swim before heading the T1.

*The Bike*: While I was swimming, Tim and Jen were well into their cycling and we were able to make contact while I was headed out and they were on their return trip. We managed to sputter out encouraging words to each other which sounded more like grunts, but the positive tones made an impact nonetheless.

While cycling, I managed to pass a few people, outdistance a pack of riders who were in hot pursuit, and hold my own on the monstrous hills found on the back end of the course. I rolled in to see Tim and Jen cheering after completing their event, along with Maggie, Alex, Claudia, Payton, Mom and Dad, Maggie's parents, Ali, Anisa, Ada, Emilia, Anna, Laken, and a few of our friends who made the trip to participate and to support each other.

In the last half-mile of a the run, I pulled from my depths enough juice to pick up the pace and bring in another 30–34 aged male who was headed for the home-stretch. Before entering the park, I put sufficient space between us to eliminate a sprint finish. This landed me fourth among my age-group and I believe thir-teenth overall.

Tim earned fourth in his age-group, and Jen claimed the top spot in her age-group, while the kids all had a great time doing the Fun Run. Ali asserted himself after being reluctant to even toe the starting line, to earn first overall and Anisa was the first *girl* to cross the finish line.

Maggie earned the "Trooper" award because she was unable to compete after a softball injury left her shin badly bruised rendering her unable to run. This was especially difficult for her since virtually all of our family was participating in something. Nevertheless, we all had a great weekend, like we always do at Otsego Lake in Gaylord, in early August.

## Three Rivers Triathlon, August 2005
## (1.5k/40k/10k)

The alarm's beep-beeping from my *Timex, Ironman* watch brought to my attention that it was time to get up, and the dark morning greeted me with dis-tant rolling thunder accompanied by periodic flashes of lightning. The forecast suggested thunderstorms in the morning and clearing in the afternoon, which was fine except I had a triathlon I wanted to do and a t-storm would either cause delays or cancellation. I slogged about the house going through the motions of preparing for a triathlon I figured wouldn't even see the start. Maggie and I had agreed ahead of time that she and the youngsters would sit this one out since the venue is not real kid-friendly and because of the threat of rain. Before I left, I let Maggie know I might be driving an hour and a half through a thunderstorm to get a t-shirt and then be sent home, or I might be gone many hours due to possi-ble delays. I was thinking the shirt might read, "*I came all the way in a thunder-storm to do the Three Rivers Triathlon, and all I got was this lousy wet t-shirt*". I know…not original, but it was on mind as I walked out the door hoping the weather would clear and the event would go on.

Jetting down US-131 it was evident I was getting closer to the storm and not further away. After the very familiar Portage Centre exit, there were times when I had to slow way down and initiate the hazard lights, while I hunched over the wheel to see the lines on the highway. I was reasonably confident I would arrive at the race site only to find a solo volunteer on site. I figured he would be shaking his head telling me to go home because the event had been cancelled, while wondering what kind of idiot I was for coming all the down in a storm. On the contrary, I reached my destination and found the parking area nearly full with hoards of people scrambling around in ponchos getting their bikes to the transition area. "Good," I thought, "I'm not the *only* idiot."

If you are a long-time recipient of the *Race Fans* reports, you know I hate to…say it with me…get my bike wet. Well, here I was parked at the event with a steady rain coming down and with uncertainty about whether or not a triathlon would take place. However, bike slots in the transition were clearly being filled rapidly and I didn't want to be left with a bogus spot if this thing got off the ground. Therefore, in efforts to preserve my bike and not lose a spot on the racks, I placed my transition rug (colorful floppy rug one might purchase for $5 at Meijer for camping etc.) down hoping my fellow athletes would accept this as my claim. I thought about writing "Dibs" on a piece of paper and taping it to a choice place on a rack, but I didn't have the materials required.

Moving forward with the preliminary preparations, I stood in various important lines: Porta-potty-line, find-your-race-number-line, gear-bag-line, body-marking-line, and I took care of these things while holding an umbrella. Of course all the while I was wondering if any of this would even be necessary. It was getting to the point where I had to get my bike out of its dry confines and out into the wretched rain, just in case the race got off the ground. As if understanding my plight, the rain slowed as I got closer to the car, and it then stopped just before I inserted the key into the door to unlock it. I gently removed my two-wheeled companion, inflated the tires, grabbed my gear bag and wetsuit, began my trek from the parking area to the race staging area and…the rain came steadily down once again. For good measure a rumble of thunder sounded in the not-so-far-off distance, and a flash of lightning cracked the now gray sky. Ok, so much for understanding.

My gear was finally set-up and strategically covered in a variety of small plastic bags, while my towel covered my bike, and to the best of its ability kept it from becoming entirely soaked. I stood in the rain in the best active wear I could find (my wetsuit) while chatting with other soaking participants waiting for the second delay to end, and with hopes of getting started. The announcement finally came at the same time as the rain went from steady, to drizzle, and then to non-existent, that there would be a race meeting at the waterfront in fifteen minutes.

All things considered, the race send-off was only an hour later than scheduled, which was pretty good. This happened unsurprisingly after race director Emil Millet was done explaining the course details in his traditional humorous, yet informative fashion, and warning us to be cautious on the now, "awfully slick roadways". The first wave was the men 39 and under, and once in the water I prepared quickly because I knew Emil's habit was to start quickly. Sure enough, he shouted out, "Are you guys ready?" then instantaneously he sounded the horn as if answering his own question. Immediately following a collective, "Oh sh@#!" we took off heading for the first buoy.

*The Swim*: I knew going in this would be my longest swim of the season, and though I was sufficiently trained to cover 1.5k at a reasonable pace, it seemed to take quite long time to complete.

*T1*: The transition set-up is long by any standards due to limited space, and as a result, my transition times were slow. In T1 it didn't help my cause that I had to take a minute to clean my rain spattered glasses before I could get going.

*The Bike*: It had been several years since I had done the Three *Rivers Triathlon* long course, and I had forgotten just how hilly it was. After a series of hills that I was familiar with from the short course, I was sent out to take on more hills. In fact, I think within the 40k bike course there was only half a mile of flat terrain. We were either climbing or descending. There were two occasions where I thought I might crash my bike. One was at the hairpin turn-around point at the 20k mark, and the other was after making a rapid descent, followed by a sharp right turn. My breaks did not respond as quickly due to conditions and I didn't realize the turn was as tight as it was. I narrowly escaped, but I knew others might not. Later I learned there were a couple of crashes, and I saw one victim whose whole left side was covered with road rash. Due to the frequency of the hills, I was changing gears almost as much as a mountain biker, and on one occasion as I was ascending a hill, my chain fell off. Instead of freaking out however, I kept peddling and changed my gears enough to bring the chain back on the rings. I ended up climbing in the big ring for that hill, but it was better than having to stop and put the chain back on. Ultimately I made it back without further incident and with a big cushion on those behind me. However, I was also keenly aware that many were ahead of me with their own cushion on me.

*T2*: Again it was time consuming in the long, narrow transition area, but after switching up for appropriate gear and shedding my singlet, I was off to do battle with more hills, competitors with a lead on me, and the exceedingly evident humidity.

*The Run*: My goal was to get out strong, settle in, and reel in anyone in my sights. I had a good start but unfortunately there was nobody in my sights until almost mile two. It was apparent that the guy in front of me was running about the same pace I was so, I had to be patient to see if he would soon waiver. As he passed one of our competitors up ahead, I knew I too would soon be overtaking the same guy, and I was slowly making up ground. After a few decent-sized hills, he was beginning to falter while my pace remained steady, and I passed with a surge to let him know I wasn't going to be taking any passengers with me. Further in the distance was Adriano Rosa, a long-time triathlete who kicks butt on a regular basis with his superior swimming and cycling prowess. I knew I would be going by him soon, but I also recognized that his wave stared several minutes after mine, and though I was passing him on the course, he was way in front of me. We exchanged "Good jobs" and I focused on two more gents on the horizon with about three-quarters of a mile to go. They were half-way up the last big-arse, 300 meter hill, and I was about that same distance behind them. I would like to say I powered up the hill like a mo-fo and smoked 'em, but I trudged up the hill pulling my butt in my little red wagon hoping they would trip on their shoe laces or something. I didn't give up hope however, because after the big uphill fight, there was a long downhill before entering the staging area. I let my legs go, sucked lots of air as my lungs burned and my heart pounded, but I was determined to catch these guys. The first one I managed to overtake just before the driveway, but the second one required still more effort as we charged up a small incline leading us into the final turn. I gave it my all with my arms and legs pumping and all cylinders firing. I nearly edged him out, but we crossed with a few meters between us with him crossing first. I pressed "stop" on the same watch that woke me up hours before and put my hands on my sweat drenched knees, and sucked air until I could stumble off with the fresh, cold water bottle the finish line volunteers had just handed me. Even though it took me about an hour to clean my dirty and wet bike when I got home, it was a good day.

## Ludington Triathlon, August 2005
### 500m/20k/5k

While preparing my space in the transition area, I paused for a moment to absorb the view around me. The early morning sun shone brightly on the cold and choppy waves on Lake Michigan, which was roughly a hundred meters from where I was standing. The sky held a multitude of colors, mostly in shades of pink and purple, but was being overtaken by the cloudless blue which was being shuttled through from the east. Ludington's City Park's beach to the north of me, and close enough to fly a kite over, was being picked clean by a few screeching seagulls, as they called dibs on their finds. A brisk west wind drifted through, but the air was pleasant. After a dark, early, and labored two-plus hour drive from Middleville, I arrived to receive my reward. This is what I do.

To prevent a major shock to my system at the start of the race, I acclimated myself to the water knowing it would take my breath away. While the waves covered only my ankles, I knew running in and taking a shallow dive was not going to happen. Though wetsuit clad, the 56-degree water made its presence known, with two-foot swells and a washing machine-like chop helping me understand that this was Lake Michigan, and not Bassett Lake. After wading waste-deep and swishing my arms around for awhile, I finally gathered the courage to submerge myself. Immediately my eyes widened, my heart rate sky-rocketed, the bare skin on my arms tightened, and I defiantly swam a few yards with each movement forward being challenged. "*Whoo!*" We've all been in water at some point in our lives that warranted this response, and this was another one of those times for me. Another brief plunge and I took to the shore where I waited for my wave (short course men) to start.

*The Swim & T1*: Normally I would prefer to start on the outer edge and ease my way into the group, but today I was feeling confident, though with no compelling reason why when considering the conditions, and the starting line found me on the innermost edge. This position required a straight shot to the first and most challenging buoy to reach. The horn sounded, so the race was underway and we bounded into the waves. I decided not to wait too long in starting my swim, so while many others continued to stay upright as long as they could, I went horizontal and started my clash with the elements. While plowing forward, it was evident I was being tossed around a bit, because I could feel the waves crashing against my head, and the fairly tame multi-directional currents attempting to pull me off course. Furthermore, at times it was difficult taking periodic glances to confirm the orange marker buoys were ahead of me.

Nearing the beach I could see athletes standing early to get out of the water, but I kept my stroke until I could touch the sandy bottom. It was difficult to determine my position in the race, because upon reaching transition there were many people scuttling about. There was a long course triathlon, as well as a duathlon being run, in addition to the short course triathlon, so it was a challenge knowing who I was directly competing against. No matter, I performed my transition ritual as quickly as I could with little resistance from my wetsuit, and I jogged my bike to the mounting point.

*The Bike*: My objective was to make the race happen for me in the saddle, so I quickly reached the cadence I wanted and headed down the smooth pavement of Ludington's *Lakeshore Drive* heading northward. From experience with the *Ludington LakestrideHaf-Marathon*, I knew the route quite well. After crossing a bridge at the bottom of a long, gradual hill, we headed up a similar hill where half-way up, the road split. This was also the point where the long course triathletes, short course triathletes, and duathletes parted ways. Unfortunately, the duathlon traversed the same route as the short course athletes, so my position in the race was still unclear.

Two athletes were peddling about a quarter of a mile ahead of me, so it was clear what my first task was. The two were only separated by 200 meters or so, and after passing the first, it did not take long to catch the next. Looking forward to a new target, I spotted a cyclist yet another 400 meters ahead, but he didn't seem to be moving quite as fast as the others. I typically think of these athletes as "Good swimmers." These are the guys (or gals) who smoke me out of the water, but are not as strong on the bike. The cross winds began catching my wider, three-spoke wheels a little, but it never became a major setback. My game face was primed as I rapidly gained on my adversary, and I began preparations to let him know this pass was as permanent as they come. Then a slow grin crept across my face, followed by a short chuckle. The "competitor" I was getting my heart rate up for was none other than a gray-haired senior attempting to keep youth in his corner during his morning spin. He may have had a basket on the front of his touring hybrid, wide-tired cruiser, but it all happened so quickly, that I'm just not sure.

Our turn-around point was marked just before *Ludington State Park*, and I could see it clearly as I jetted downhill, while adjusting my gears for the inclined return. There had been no cyclists headed back toward town, so it was at this point I acknowledged that I was the leader. I was pushing the pace to get back and my pursuers were going the opposite direction while approaching the turn-around. I knew it was my race to lose. To stay focused on my pace, I imagined I was in second and the leader was too far in front for me to view, and that I had to work to get him in my sights to chase him down.

*T2*: Apparently a large silver pick-up managed to get by the race volunteers, and on its way to the parking lot, he pulled right in front of me at a very low speed. As indicated by the skid marks left on the pavement, it is clear to me that my brakes work. Fortunately this was only a temporary setback, and I was able to dismount, get my running gear, and set out to continue what I started. While exiting the transition, my nearest two competitors came in sight while entering T1. For them however, it was slow-moving-truck, obstruction free.

*The Run*: With a target on my back and unaware of how fleet-of-foot my competitors were, I had to be strong, but not take off like a scared rabbit, only to be later caught and eaten by the more patient fox. Again I was in familiar territory running along Ludington's City Park. I knew I wasn't breaking any 5k records, but I held a steady pace. After the turn-around at the bridge, marking the half-way point of the run, I finally I dared take inventory of my stalkers. I immediately spotted the current runner-up headed down the hill leading to the volunteer who was directing us back to town. Fear was suddenly a source of fuel. I surged up the hill, so by the time my challenger completed the turn-around, he might believe I was too far ahead to be reeled in. I didn't look back to determine whether or not my tactic was a success, I just kept telling myself to keep it on.

As I approached the entrance to the park, I asked a group of on-lookers how far back the next guy was. The response was what I wanted to hear, but it wasn't enough, because they shouted, "Oh, he's a ways back." O.K. What's "a ways back"? I began thinking, "Was it a smidgen? Perhaps it was a tad? Possibly it was a dash or a bit? People…work with me here! Is he 200 meters, 400 meters…what? Take a guess!" I know, that was a bit harsh, uncalled for, and of course was not expressed verbally. The turn into the park did not allow for much over-the-shoulder peering, so I still didn't know how close this guy was and I was running out of real estate. Was this going to be a sprint finish to see who had the most guts? Could this guy come cruising around the corner, put the big hurt on me, and leave me babbling along the lakeshore, as he raised his hands in victory after crossing the finish line?

The last 500 meters was something the race director was especially proud of, and for good reason. What he had created was a nice touch to make things inter-esting and more challenging. Upon entering the park, I was sent down the beach to the shoreline. I ran on as much wet packed sand as possible without getting my feet wet. With about 150 meters left to go, I came across another set of people, and I checked their ability to give me the low-down on what was happening behind me. They told me what I *really* wanted to hear, with a wide open beach, on a clear day. They said, "He's nowhere in sight!" Thank goodness too, because heading back up the beach toward the parking lot/finish line area was an uphill battle in the sand. This was far more challenging than the trip down to the water-front. My arms were pumping, my legs were churning, and my heart was pound-ing while my lungs burned, and my pace reminded me of an older guy I saw earlier on his bike. I told myself, "It's not over 'till it's over." Then I finally reached the crest of the sand hill and took to the pavement where I might have heard a sound like squealing tires at the moment shoes made contact. The next thing I heard was Kenny from *3D Racing* over the P.A., *"Finishing first in the Ludington Short Course Triathlon is Sam Wilkinson, from Middleville, Michigan! Great job Sam!"* That's when I knew it was over.

After discarding my timing chip, accepting my finisher's medal and small cold, wet towel, and grabbing my knees, as I sucked air for a while, I looked around. About 150 meters from me was the chilly waters of Lake Michigan, with the sun dancing on the still restless waves. The beach now blemished with blotches of sunbathers accompanied by screeching seagulls who were still looking for items in which to stake their claim. The sky had become completely overwhelmed by blue, and the day went on.

Walking back to the van with my full backpack strapped to my shoulders and pushing my bike, as well as carrying our youngest in my free arm, Payton said, "Daddy…you're a fast runner." I was keenly reminded at this point, that this is not *all* that I do.

## Reeds Lake Triathlon, September 2005 (.5mi/18mi/5mi)

In the week or so leading up to the *Reeds Lake Triathlon,* I was feeling fatigued and ready for a break from competition, but still two goals for this event lingered. Finishing in the top fifteen I decided would be excellent for me, and I knew that it would require a stellar performance, but it was still something that was in my sights. I determined twentieth place or better would be a respectable feat, and any place thereafter would be acceptable. My next goal was to produce a time under 1:31:00, which again would be a challenge, but it was a reasonable one. The day started cool, but not cold, and it carried a light breeze, but it wasn't windy. The water was calm and wetsuit legal, and the sun was revealing a cloudless sky. The field of over 725 people was rich with talent and the stage was set for great things to happen, so there were no excuses. It was up to me to make it happen.

After previously thinking Maggie and our children would be unable to attend because of a soccer game and dance practice, it was realized that if after I finished, I quickly grabbed my gear and we rushed off, we could fit it all in. So, once again we answered the call to get up early on a Saturday morning before the sun was here, and we rushed around our house filing sippy-cups, putting *Froot Loops* in baggies, and making sure every child had his or her beloved items. Finally with our 1996, green Plymouth Grand Voyager mini-van filled with the necessities of the day, we set out.

Because I registered the night before, I had two less lines to stand in, and because I have my personal pre-race protocol down, I made the critical porta-jon stop at just the right time to avoid yet another line. Some seem to think it is more important to set up their transition area first and attend to *bitness* later. I hope this thinking continues, because I can relax and arrange my gear in transition while others stand in line anxiety stricken, not knowing whether they will be able to open the door of to one of the Superman changing stations with a toilet before the start.

Doing a mental checklist is important prior to leaving the transition area to prepare for the swim. I imagined myself doing each of the disciplines and I pictured myself equipped with what I needed. While I did this, I looked and checked to see if I had available the items I was viewing in my head. If I was missing something I would have needed to locate the item or items immediately. Fortunately, I go through this the night before events as well, and I have only forgotten my earplugs once. This was far less tragic than if I had forgotten my helmet, cycling shoes, or Heaven help me, my bike. Of course the day I forget my bike is the day I resign from triathlon…However, everything was in its place.

After feeling good about my gear arrangement, it was time to warm-up. I headed for the lakefront clad in my superhero outfit, which consists of my wetsuit, swimcap, goggles, and earplugs. When I'm decked out in this way, *Batman* has no fashion edge on *me*. I wasted little time getting in the water and it was a good way to wake-up and to get my blood flowing.

After exiting the water, I wondered around without my glasses squinting to find Maggie with our crew in tow. Almost immediately after finding them Maggie asked, "Hey, isn't that Coach Soderman?" I was only somewhat surprised to see him, but mostly anxious to give him his due. I quickly walked over toward him, "Coach Soderman!" In his typical friendly fashion he replied, "Hey, Sam, how you doing?" He informed me his daughter was participating and she was preparing for the swim. What a rush it was to hear Coach's voice and know he would be here while I was competing. I returned to Maggie, and she and the kids gave me good luck wishes, hugs, and kisses, and I finally realized the men of the second wave were all standing on the shore like they were about to start. This of course was *my* wave so I had to hustle. I shuffled through where athletes were being counted and ran to the water expecting the horn to sound before I arrived. A familiar face, in Chris VanRyan (former Caledonian) greeted me and I heard the announcement that we had a minute before the start. Normally I would be more on the ball with my start, but I didn't hear the first wave horn sound.

*The Swim & T1*: "Counting down from 10, 9, 8…" the starter shouted, "7, 6…" I was ready and confident. The time was now and my intention was to give this race all of what I had to offer. I just didn't yet know what that would be. "…2, 1..*BURNNNT!*" The countdown ended, the horn sounded, I quickly pushed "Start" on my watch and rushed into the water and the depth allowed me to start swimming almost immediately. The sun by this time was nearly blinding as it rested on the opposite shore, and it was difficult to sight. My strokes were rapid-but-controlled, and fortunately so was my breathing, which allowed me to make good progress early. After a while I noticed that not only was I passing the navy blue caps that were in my wave, but also the white caps of the first wave. "Cool," I thought, "I caught the first wave!" This was a confidence booster as I headed for the sun and hoped not to pass the large orange buoy telling me to turn, as a result of the severe glare on the water and blasting rays. I found it, and I rounded it...no worries. I kept it on, and started questioning if I was giving too much to the swim, but decided to take the chance, and I didn't back off my pace. Occasionally sneaking glances ahead of me, I spotted the colorful shore with the hoards of spectators in their array of sweatshirts, hats, and baby joggers. I was smiling wide on the inside, but remained steady and on task on the outside. I broke the water and began climbing the cement boat launch leading to the transition area. I hustled past the generous few who elected to walk from the water to their bikes, and found my biggest fans standing just outside the "Police Line Do Not Cross" tape which formed the transition area. "Go daddy!" As quickly as I could, I transformed from swimmer to cyclist and trotted cautiously in my cycling shoes while towing my bike out to the mounting point, just outside the transition area. As a rule I hit the "Lap" button on my watch to record my splits, but today only one time mattered. Pushing "Stop" at the finish line would be the next and last button I would push at today's event.

*The Bike*: Once I was clipped in my pedals, I was rolling and looking to take no prisoners while on two wheels. Weeks prior to arriving, it was my intent to wreak havoc on the bike and let my competitors know I was no punk, and that winning the *Ludington Short Course Triathlon* didn't mean I couldn't or wouldn't toe the line with the big boys. Of course the reality was that the only one paying attention to this line of thinking was me, so this showing of machismo was only in my head for additional motivation. Truly, nobody else noticed or cared whether or not I won a short course event, or bothered to question whether or not I had the goods to put it together against the heavy hitters. Nevertheless, I projected this upon every cyclist I approached.

Because I was sifting through the tail-end of the first wave, I was passing people readily and all the while trying not to allow myself to believe I was making serious headway in the race. I recognized there were many competitors ahead of me to catch, and regardless of the fact that we couldn't see each other, those who started the race in a wave after me were in pursuit.

Within about five miles of the bike I was cruising along Fulton, and I noticed a guy in a red jersey ahead of me and traveling about the same pace as me. I thought of him as "Red Guy" and set my sights on him rather than the few athletes that separated us. I knew among those I could see, he was the man to beat. Patiently I reeled him in while leaving others behind, and then I put in a merciless surge while attempting to put pavement between us once I caught him. He was taken back a little because I think he was used to being "The Man" and he didn't expect to be passed. He didn't take being passed lightly, and he produced an admirable counterpunch within a half-mile to let me know he wasn't going away easily, and his ride cruised by mine. No looks or pleasantries were exchanged. None were needed. We understood each other's language very clearly. Without a word, he stated plainly that he was "The Man" and I let him know that I didn't care. Though he remained in front of me heading to the turn-around cones at the bottom of the hill, I had a plan to regain my position over him. I shifted from my big ring to my small ring and set myself up to get out of the blocks quickly, after taking the turn that caused us to nearly come to a stop. I got out of my saddle and cranked up the RPMs while he struggled in his big ring with slow grinding turns of the pedals. The result was another pass by the skinny guy on the *Litespeed*. Almost instantly we had to ascend a long hill, and I was will-ing myself through time and space trying to convince this guy he was not "The Man" he thought he was. Near the crest of the hill however, he informed me, by way of giving me a full view of his black, Pearl Izumi, Tri-shorts ass, that he indeed *was* "The Man," and he left me his proverbial business card that read as much. Though temporarily broken, I kept him in my sights.

Another player entered the scene sporting a black Felt ride and cruising at speeds strong enough to hang with "Red Guy" for a while. Naturally, I had to go after him. I couldn't let both "Red Guy" and "Felt" become thieves of my thun-der. We whipped through the curved streets that surrounded the backside of Reeds Lake, and though I could no longer see "Red Guy" as we began the ascent of the infamous "Hall Street Hill," I had "Felt" in my sights and wasn't letting go. A crowd had formed at the top of the hill to direct traffic and cheer on their ath-letes, and they provided us with their support. It was no *Tour De France* mind you, but I took the love nonetheless. Whether "Hall Street Hill" zapped "Felt" or he was spent from covering the course almost in its entirety, he had nothing to respond with when I finally overtook him before turning on to Lake Drive. "Red Guy" could have been feeling the effects of his strong bike effort, or he began to preserve his energy for the run, or I was simply feeling fresh enough to catch him, but whatever the reason was we hit the dismount line at the same time.

*T2*: Quick in and quick out.

*The Run*: I set out alone not knowing where "Red Guy" was and I began look-ing in front of me to chase him down, or anyone else I could see. However, I ran virtually alone for the first mile, not sure how far in front of me "Red Guy" was. As it turned out, I beat him out of transition and he was stalking me the whole time, and after I downed the cool water from the *Gatorade* paper cup given to me by a generous volunteer, he eased by my left shoulder while he took his new posi-tion in the race. He was on a mission, and as I slowly chewed a few bites of hum-ble pie ala-mode, the gap between us became insurmountable. I took another slice from the pie tin when only moments later "Felt" passed me. He pulled away, but motioned with his hand for me to go with him, but I knew I wasn't boarding his train.

The last mile was calming after I looked over my shoulder while rounding a turn and saw nobody near me, and then looked forward accepting I was not going to catch anyone in front of me, because nobody was in sight. I cruised along at a respectable, but not blistering pace, and took in the sights and sounds of what made the *Reeds Lake Triathlon*. I noticed that the last aid station consisted of a troop of *Boy Scouts of America*. I figured a community service merit badge was being well earned today. Small children were sitting on the curb eating ice cream and occasionally shouting out encouraging words to the inhabitants that took over their streets for the morning. Then I noticed the intersection I had taken in so many times before by way of the many *Resolution Runs, Reeds Lake Runs*, and of course this event. A sense of pride and accomplishment came over me while galloping by the East Grand Rapids Middle School Parking Lot on my right, and the high school track on my left. This marked the beginning of the end. This was the final stretch, and I could see and hear people I know on the not-so-distant top of the slight hill I was climbing. My pace quickened somewhat, my posture was sharpened, and the need to motor down the final 300 meters of pavement along Collins Park was exceptionally high. "Let's go Sam!" the familiar voice of former *Gazelle Sports* co-worker and friend Mike (Gorkowski) rang out, and I veered over to the sidewalk where he stood and I held up my hand for the high-five I needed to give and receive. The crowd along the street was large, as it is traditionally, and I could hear the cheers and the support clearly. Furthermore, I knew Coach was looking on somewhere in the mass. I was totally in the moment. "Way to go Sam," I heard my dad shout from the sidewalk where he was assisting Maggie in corralling our children, and I floated across the finish line where I finally pushed "Stop" on my watch. I shook the hands of the few who recently preceded me, which included "Red Guy" and "Felt," with a smile on my face, and they knew I respected that they were the better men that day. After a moment of further catching my breath, I looked at my watch; the watch with only one split. It read 1:30:56.

I had to be pleased with the outcome. I was the 20th overall finisher, fifth among 30–34 aged males, and I met my goal of going under 1:31:00. I also discovered I own the 15th fastest bike split on the day. The *Reeds Lake Triathlon* is not my end-all-be-all race, but it is fulfilling to do well in a race with such a large volume of competitors who do see it as such. It's very satisfying to finish another triathlon season on a positive note. I love this sport!

# Epilogue

*"I'd rather burn out than rust."*—Joan Benoit (1983)

Though I am taking a moment to celebrate the last ten years of participation in triathlon and related events, I have no intention of staying on the porch while the big dogs run by. I will continue to adjust my goggles before entering the cool waters of Bassett Lake, or before chasing the black line in the TKHS pool. I will continue to clasp the strap on my helmet prior to putting rubber to the road, as I cycle along the rolling hills of Barry County. I will continue to tighten my laces before braving the heat or cold that Michigan weather offers, giving my *Saucony* running shoes a chance to do their thing. I will continue to toe the lines of triathlons, duathlons, time trials, foot races, and so forth, and I will share my experiences with the *Race Fans* who have been with me all along. I will keep going until I can go no longer, because I will not just sit down and rust when I can keep moving. *Here's to the next ten years!*

# Appendix

## High School Cross Country Times
## 1985–1988

| Race | Venue | Year | Time |
|---|---|---|---|
| EGR & Lakewood | Lakeside Park | 1985 | 19:38 |
| Lowell & Unity Christian | Lakeside Park | 1985 | 18:59 |
| TK Invitational | Gun Lake | 1985 | 19:01 |
| Forest Hills Northern | Lakeside Park | 1985 | 19:45 |
| Byron Center | Douglass Walker Pk. | 1985 | 23:42 |
| Lee | Douglass Walker Pk. | 1985 | 19:38 |
| Fennville Invitational | Fennville | 1985 | 18:20 |
| Hamilton | Douglass Walker Pk. | 1985 | 19:24 |
| Lowell Invitational | Lowell | 1985 | 20:58 |
| Godwin | Douglass Walker Pk. | 1985 | 19:36 |
| Middleville/TK | Douglass Walker Pk. | 1985 | 19:40 |
| Rockford Invitational | Pando Ski Area | 1985 | 21:17 |
| Comstock Park | Douglass Walker Pk. | 1985 | 19:14 |
| O.K. Blue Conference/JV | Douglass Walker Pk. | 1985 | 18:53 |
| Race | Venue | Year | Time |
| Coopersville | Lakeside Park | 1986 | 21:29 |
| Lowell & Unity Christian | Lakeside Park | 1986 | 17:19 |
| TK Invitational | Gun Lake | 1986 | 18:19 |
| Forest Hills Northern | Lakeside Park | 1986 | 18:26 |
| Lee | Douglass Walker Pk. | 1986 | 18:21 |
| Hamilton | Douglass Walker Pk. | 1986 | 19:19 |
| Fennville Invitational | Fennville | 1986 | 18:15 |
| Godwin | Douglass Walker Pk. | 1986 | 18:05 |

| Race | Venue | Year | Time |
|------|-------|------|------|
| Lowell Invitational | Lowell | 1986 | 20:35 |
| Middleville/TK | Douglass Walker Pk. | 1986 | 18:41 |
| Comstock Park | Douglass Walker Pk. | 1986 | 17:47 |
| Rockford Invitational | Pando Ski Area | 1986 | 18:08 |
| Byron Center | Douglass Walker Pk. | 1986 | 17:50 |
| OK Blue conference | Douglass Walker Pk. | 1986 | 17:58 |
| Class "B" Regional | CRC Rec. Area | 1986 | 17:32 |
| Class "B" State | | 1986 | 17:35 |
| Race | Venue | Year | Time |
| EGR & Coopersville | Lakeside Park | 1987 | 17:16 |
| Lowell & Unity | Lakeside Park | 1987 | 17:02 |
| FHN & Hopkins | Lakeside Park | 1987 | 17:13 |
| TK Invitational | Gun Lake | 1987 | 18:40 |
| Olivet Invitational | Olivet | 1987 | 17:28 |
| Lee | Brewer Park | 1987 | 18:38 |
| Fennville Invitational | Fennville | 1987 | 17:04 |
| Hamilton | Brewer Park | 1987 | 18:21 |
| Godwin | Brewer Park | 1987 | 17:38 |
| Middleville/TK | Brewer Park | 1987 | 17:50 |
| Rockford Invitational | Pando Ski Area | 1987 | 18:03 |
| Comstock Park | Brewer Park | 1987 | 18:12 |
| Byron Center | Brewer Park | 1987 | 17:21 |
| Alumni Meet | Lakeside Park | 1987 | 17:20 |
| Kellogsville | Brewer Park | 1987 | 18:22 |
| OK Blue Conference | Brewer Park | 1987 | 17:48 |
| Class "B" Regional | CRC Rec. Area | 1987 | 17:48 |
| Class "B" State | | 1987 | 17:30 |
| Race | Venue | Year | Time |
| EGR | Lakeside Park | 1988 | 16:41 |
| Lowell & Unity Christian | Lakeside Park | 1988 | 16:44 |
| Cedar Springs | Johnson Park | 1988 | 17:45 |
| TK Invitational | Gun Lake | 1988 | 17:10 |
| Hudsonville | Johnson Park | 1988 | 17:57 |
| Olivet Invitational | Olivet | 1988 | 17:09 |
| South Christian | Johnson Park | 1988 | 17:26 |

| Race | Venue | Year | Time |
|---|---|---|---|
| Fennville Invitational | Fennville | 1988 | 17:04 |
| Forest Hills Northern | Johnson Park | 1988 | 17:26 |
| Alumni Meet | Lakeside Park | 1988 | 16:50 |
| Wayland | Johnson Park | 1988 | 17:52 |
| Rockford Invitational | Pando Ski Area | 1988 | 18:41 |
| Coopersville | Johnson Park | 1988 | 17:29 |
| Kenowa Hills | Johnson Park | 1988 | 17:41 |
| OK GOLD Conference | Johnson Park | 1988 | 17:34 |
| Bronco Classic | Johnson Park | 1988 | 19:10 |
| Class "B" Regional | CRC Rec. Area | 1988 | 18:41 |

## College Cross Country Times
## Grand Rapids Junior College 1989–1990
## Grand Valley State University 1991–1992

| Grand Rapids Junior College: Fall 1989 | | |
|---|---|---|
| Calvin Invitational | 8k | 29:19 |
| Aquinas Dual | 8k | 32:21 |
| Ferris Invitational | 8k | 27:57 |
| Macomb Invitational | 8k | 29:44 |
| SMC Invitational | 8k | 28:22 |
| GVSU Invitational | 8k | 30:20 |
| NJCAA Regional (LCC) | 8k | 29:03 |
| | | |
| Grand Rapids Junior College: Fall 1990 | | |
| GVSU Invitational | 8k | 28:44 |
| Calvin Invitational | 8k | 28:15 |
| Ferris Invitational | 8k | 28:21 |
| SMC Invitational | 8k | 28:30 |
| GVSU Invitational II | 5k | 17:47 |
| GRJC Invitational | 8k | 28:38 |
| NJCAA Regional (SMC) | 8k | 27:38 |
| | | |
| Grand Valley State University: Fall 1991 | | |
| GVSU Invitational | 8k | 29:47 |
| Hope Invitational | 8k | 28:56 |
| Ferris Dual (GVSU) | 8k | 28:41 |
| Kenosha Championships | 8k | 28:22 |
| Ferris Invitational | 8k | 28:35 |
| SMC Invitational | 8k | 27:16 |
| M.I.C. Ypsilanti | 8k | 27:42 |
| GVSU Invitational II | 5k | 16:44 |
| GLIAC Championship | 10k | 37:39 |
| | | |

| Grand Valley State University: Fall 1992 | | |
|---|---|---|
| Hope Invitational | 8k | 27:47 |
| Ferris Dual (GVSU) | 8k | 28:33 |
| Kenosha Championships | 8k | 28:06 |
| Ferris Invitational | 8k | 27:45 |
| SMC Invitational | 8k | 27:45 |
| M.I.C. Shepherd | 8k | 28:19 |
| GVSU Invitational II | 5k | 16:59 |
| GLIAC Championship | 10k | 37:18 |
| NCAA Division II | 10k | 36:16 |

## Races of All Types
## 1989–2005

| Event | Distance | Time |
|---|---|---|
| **1989** | | |
| Plainwell Classic | 5k | 17:30 |
| Grand Haven Coast Guard Festival | 10k | 39:09 |
| **1990** | | |
| Grand Rapids, Irish Jig | 5k | 17:24 |
| Jenison, Memorial Day Run | 10k | 36:40 |
| Ludington, Lakestride | 10k | 36:03 |
| E. Grand Rapids, Reeds Lake Run | 10k | 36:09 |
| Allegan, Perrigo Run | 5k | 17:00 |
| Middleville, Turkey Trot | 10k | 34:42 |
| **1991** | | |
| E. Grand Rapids, Resolution Run | 4 mile | 22:40 |
| Grand Rapids, Irish Jig | 5k | 17:27 |
| Allegan, April Fool Run | 5k | 17:25 |
| Grand Haven, Snug Harbor Run | 5k | 17:04 |
| Kalamazoo, Kalamazoo Classic | 10k | 36:42 |
| Plainwell, Plainwell Classic | 10k | 36:10 |
| Ironwood, Interstate Run | 10k | 36:29 |
| **1992** | | |
| Grand Rapids, Irish Jig | 5k | 17:07 |
| Holland, Tulip Time Run | 20k | 1:17:37 |
| E. Grand Rapids, Reeds Lake Run | 5k | 17:32 |
| Flint, Crim Festival of Races | 10 mile | 59:02 |
| Dutton, Tricks or Treats Run | 5k | 16:14 |
| Grand Rapids, Save Our Sports Run | 5k | 16:18 |
| **1993** | | |
| E. Grand Rapids, Resolution Run | 4 mile | 24:00 |
| Grand Rapids, Irish Jig | 5k | 16:36 |
| Grand Rapids, Old Kent Riverbank Run | 5k | 18:11 |
| Ludington, Ludington Lakestride | 10k | 36:57 |
| Grandville, Buck Creek Run | 5 mile | 30:34 |
| Grand Haven Coast Guard Festival | 5k | 16:32 |
| Allegan, Perrigo Run | 10k | 35:38 |
| Hastings Summerfest Run | 5k | 16:22 |
| Caledonia, Cross Country Alumni Meet | 5k | 16:47 |
| Zeeland, Bil Mar Turkey Trot | 5k | 16:34 |
| Detroit Free Press International Marathon | 26.2 | 3:15:38 |

| Event | Distance | Time |
|---|---|---|
| E. Grand Rapids, Run Thru Apple Country | 5k | 17:04 |
| Dutton, Tricks or Treats Run | 5k | 16:55 |
| Kalamazoo, KTC Cross Country Run | 5k | 17:50 |
| **1994** | | |
| E. Grand Rapids, Resolution Run | 4 mile | 25:00 |
| GVSU, Indoor Track Meet | 5k | 16:24 |
| S. Carolina, Marathon & 10k | 10k | 34:56 |
| Grand Rapids, Irish Jig | 5k | 16:32 |
| Whitehall, Channel to Channel Run | 20k | 1:16:28 |
| Pinckney, Michigan Trail ½ Marathon | 13.1 mile | 1:31:30 |
| Ludington Lakestride ½ Marathon | 13.1 mile | 1:27:02 |
| Flint, Crim Festival of Races | 10 mile | 58:37 |
| Cannonsberg Ski, Harrier Cross Country Run | 5k | 18:02 |
| Zeeland, Bil Mar Turkey Trot | 5k | 16:34 |
| Detroit Free Press International Marathon | 26.2 mile | 3:13:09 |
| E. Grand Rapids, Run Thru Apple Country Run | 5k | 17:54 |
| **1995** | | |
| E. Grand Rapids, Resolution Run | 4 mile | 24:58 |
| Traverse City, Cherry Festival Run | 5k | 18:32 |
| Grand Haven Coast Guard Festival | 5k | 18:00 |
| *Gaylord, Mark Mellon Triathlon (Short Course) FIRST TRIATHLON* | 200yd/10mi/2mi | 51:47 |
| Grand Rapids, Thanksgiving Day Run (with Ang) | 5k | 25:00 |
| **1996** | | |
| Lansing, Michigan Run | 5k | 17:37 |
| E. Grand Rapids, Reeds Lake Run (with Jen) | 10k | 58:55 |
| U.P. Lake Antoine Triathlon | .6mi/22mi/5mi | 1:55:42 |
| Kalamazoo, Seahorse Triathlon (short course) | .5k/15k/5k | 57:34 |
| Jackson, Clark Lake Triathlon | .5mi/13mi/4mi | 1:20:56 |
| Grand Haven Coast Guard Festival | 5k | 17:35 |
| E. Grand Rapids, Reeds Lake Triathlon | .5mi/18mi/5mi | 1:33:11 |
| E. Grand Rapids, Run Thru Apple Country Run | 10k | 38:47 |
| Kentwood, Indoor Triathlon | 15 min. each discipline | 14,472.2 yards |

| Event | Distance | Time |
|---|---|---|
| **1997** | | |
| E. Grand Rapids, Resolution Run | 4 mile | 24:53 |
| Grand Rapids, Old Kent Riverbank Run | 25k | 1:41:57 |
| Jenison, Georgetown Triathlon | .6mi/20mi/4.7mi | 1:38:16 |
| Columbus, OH, Wendy's International Triathlon | .5mi/18.5mi/4mi | 1:31:58 |
| Grandville, Buck Creek Run | 5 mile | 29:15 |
| Jackson, Clark Lake Triathlon | .5mi/13mi/4mi | 1:18:11 |
| Gaylord, Mark Mellon Triathlon | 1k/50k/10k | 2:28:56 |
| Niles Triathlon | .5mi/17.5mi/5mi | 1:33:25 |
| Allegan Cross Country Run | 5k | 18:32 |
| Middleville Turkey Trot | 5k | 18:29 |
| **1998** | | |
| E. Grand Rapids, Resolution Run | 4 mile | 24:15 |
| Grand Rapids, Old Kent Riverbank Run | 25k | 1:41:50 |
| Holland, Lake Macatowa Triathlon | .5mi/22.8mi/4.8mi | 1:49:55 |
| E. Grand Rapids, Reeds Lake Run | 10k | 36:56 |
| Kalamazoo, Seahorse Triathlon | 2k/40k/10k | 2:19:42 |
| Gaylord, Mark Mellon Triathlon | 1k/50k/10k | 2:22:55 |
| Three Rivers Triathlon | 1k/40k/10k | 2:10:17 |
| Kentwood, Grand Duathlon | 5k/30k/5k | 1:30:10 |
| Allegan Cross Country Run | 5k | 18:12 |
| Middleville Turkey Trot | 10k | 37:37 |
| **1999** | | |
| E. Grand Rapids, Resolution Run | 4 mi | 27:11 |
| Grand Rapids, Irish Jig | 5k | 17:58 |
| Ann Arbor, National City ½ Marathon | 13.1 mile | 1:29:05 |
| Holland, Lake Macatowa Triathlon | .5mi/22.8mi/4.8mi | 1:46:22 |
| Kalamazoo, Seahorse Triathlon | 2k/40k/10k | 2:35:35 |
| Jackson, Clark Lake Triathlon | .5mi/13mi/4mi | 1:17:08 |
| Gaylord, Mark Mellon Triathlon | 1k/50k/10k | 2:29:27 |
| Three Rivers Triathlon | 1k/40k/10k | 2:15:01 |
| Hastings Summerfest Run | 10k | 37:18 |
| Niles Triathlon | .5mi/17.5mi/5mi | 1:32:02 |
| Kentwood, Grand Duathlon | 5k/30k/5k | 1:27:12 |

| Event | Distance | Time |
|---|---|---|
| **2000** | | |
| E. Grand Rapids, Resolution Run | 4 mile | 24:26 |
| Pinckney, Michigan Trail ½ Marathon | 13.1 mile | 1:35:37 |
| Kalamazoo, Seahorse Duathlon | 5k/40k/10k | 2:09:23 |
| Pinckney, Pizzaman Duathlon | 2mi/14mi/4.5mi | 1:25:31 |
| Ludington Lakestride ½ Marathon | 13.1 mile | 1:23:38 |
| Jackson, Clark Lake Triathlon | .5mi/13mi/4mi | 1:16:30 |
| Gaylord, Mark Mellon Triathlon | 1k/50k/10k | 2:20:36 |
| Millersport, OH, The Great Buckeye Challenge ½ Ironman | 1.2mi/56mi/13.1mi | 5:06:06 |
| E. Grand Rapids, Reeds Lake Triathlon | .5mi/18mi/5mi *\* Short run course.* | 1:28:07\* |
| Kentwood, Grand Duathlon | 5k/30k/5k | 1:28:07 |
| Middleville Turkey Trot | 10k | 37:38 |
| **2001** | | |
| Holland, Lake Macatawa Triathlon | .5mi/22.8mi/4.8mi | 1:50:47 |
| E. Grand Rapids, Reeds Lake Run | 10k | 38:16 |
| Kalamazoo, Seahorse Triathlon | 2k/40k/10k (short swim measurement) | 2:08:37 |
| Gun Lake, Great Lakes Triathlon | .5mi/18mi/4mi | 1:23:40 |
| Gaylord, Mark Mellon Triathlon | 1k/50k/10k | 2:20:43 |
| Millersport, OH, The Great Buckeye Challenge ½ Ironman | 1.2mi/56mi/13.1mi | 5:19:12 |
| Niles Triathlon | .5mi/17.5mi/5mi | 1:31:10 |
| Kentwood, Grand Duathlon (bike only) | 30k | 48:58 |
| Middleville Turkey Trot | 5k | 20:32 |
| **2002** | | |
| Ludington Lakestride | 5k | 19:45 |
| E. Grand Rapids, Reeds Lake Run (with Maggie) | 5k | 21:39 |
| Kalamazoo, Seahorse Triathlon (short course) | .5k/20k/5k | 1:01:38 |
| Traverse City Cherry Triathlon | 1.5k/42k/10k | 2:34:05 |
| Gun Lake, Great Lakes Triathlon (course change) | .5mi/18mi/4mi | 1:31:59 |
| Gaylord, Mark Mellon Triathlon | 1k/50k/10k | 2:20:41 |
| Oscoda, Paul Bunyan ½ Ironman | 1.2mi/56mi/13.1mi | 4:53:00 |
| Kentwood, Grand Duathlon | 5k/30k/5k (course change) | 1:31:59 |
| Middleville Turkey Trot | 5k | 19:36 |

| Event | Distance | Time |
|---|---|---|
| **2003** | | |
| Grand Rapids, 5/3 Riverbank Run | 25k | 1:46:44 |
| Nelsonville, OH, Adventure Race | Various | 4:24:48 |
| Pinckney, Ann Arbor Duathlon | 2mi/14mi/5mi | 1:23:31 |
| Kalamazoo, Seahorse Triathlon | 1.5k/40k/10k | 2:21:33 |
| Muncie IN, Endurathon ½ Ironman | 1.2mi/56mi/13.1mi | 5:08:10 |
| Barlow Lake, Great Lakes Duathlon | 2mi/18mi/4.8mi | 1:27:21 |
| Gaylord, Mark Mellon Duathlon | 5k/50k/5k | 1:56:47 |
| Richland, Shermanator Triathlon | 1.5k/40k/10k | 2:07:09 |
| Niles Duathlon | 5k/17.5mi/5mi | 1:34:46 |
| E. Grand Rapids, Reeds Lake Triathlon | .5mi/18mi/5mi | 1:31:46 |
| **2004** | | |
| Holland, Lake Macatawa Triathlon | .5mi/22.8mi/4.8mi | 1:52:12 |
| Middleville, 24-Hour Challenge | Cycling first loop (126 mi) | 8 hours |
| Jackson, Clark Lake Triathlon | .5mi/13mi/4mi | 1:19:55 |
| Racine, WI, Spirit of Racine ½ Ironman | 1.2mi/56mi/13.1mi | 5:16:05 |
| Gaylord, Mark Mellon Triathlon (short course) | 200yd/11mi/3mi | 48:00 |
| Three Rivers Triathlon (short course) | 300m/20k/5k | 57:23 |
| **2005** | | |
| Middleville, 24-Hour Challenge | Cycling first & second loop (150+ miles) | |
| Ann Arbor, Waterloo Triathlon | .5mi/16mi/5mi | 1:40:24 |
| Interlochen Triathlon (short course) | 500m/20k/5k | 1:05:57 |
| Barlow Lake, Great Lakes Triathlon | .5mi/18mi/4.8mi | 1:32:40 |
| Gaylord, Mark Mellon Triathlon | 1k/50k/10k | 2:18:29 |
| Three Rivers Triathlon | 1.5k/40k/10k | 2:19:06 |
| Ludington Triathlon (short course) | 500m/20k/5k | 1:04:11 |
| Reeds Lake Triathlon | .5mi/18mi/5mi | 1:30:56 |
| Saugatauk, Mt. Baldhead Challenge | 15k | 1:03:02 |

# Resources For Triathlon

GOODS AND SERVICES:
- **De Soto Sport**—www.desotosport.com
- **Dick's Sports** (GU & Cliff Bars $0.99 each)
- **Gazelle Sports**—www.gazellesports.com
- **Nashbar**—www.nashbar.com
- **Performance Bike**—www.performancebike.com
- **Swim Outlet**—www.swimoutlet.com
- **Tri Sports**—www.trisports.com
- **Tri-zone**—www.tri-zone.com
- **Village Bike Shop**—www.villagebikeshop.com
- **Weather Report**—www.weather.com

GREAT BRANDS (Tried & True):

## Swimming
Quintana Roo (wetsuits)
Speedo (rubber earplugs)
TYR (swimwear, tri-suits, & goggles)

## Cycling
Blackburn (tire pump)           Louis Garnau (helmet)
Carnac (cycling shoes)          LOOK (pedals & carbon forks)
Cateye (cyclocomputer)          Mavic (wheels)
Continental (tires & tubes)     Michelin (tires & tubes)
HED (racing wheels)             Oakley (eyewear)
Litespeed (bicycles)            Pearl Izumi (apparel)
                                Specialized (bicycles)

## Running
Oakley (eyewear)     Pearl Izumi (apparel)     Saucony (shoes)

## Training and Racing Nutrition
Cliff Bar (before, during, or after)
Gatorade (before, during, or after)
GU (before or during)

GREAT EVENT CONTACTS:
*3-Disciplines Michigan Points Series Events—www.3disciplines.com*
*HFP Racing—www.hfpracing.com*
*Michigan Grand Prix Series—www.cooltri.com*

GREAT MAGAZINES:
*Bicycling*                              *Runner's World*
*Inside Triathlon*                       *Triathlete*

VALUABLE BOOKS:
Berhardt, Gale (2000). *Training Plans For Multisport Athletes.*
Edwards, Sally (2001). *The Complete Book of Triathlons.*
Fitzgerald, Matt (2003). *Complete Triathlon Book, The Training, Diet, Health, Equipment, And Safety Tips You Need To Do Your Best.*
Micheli, Lyle J., MD; Jenkins, Mark (1996). *Healthy Runner's Handbook.*
Noakes, Tim, MD (1991). *Lore Of Running, Discover The Science And Spirit Of Running.*
Town, Glen; Kearney, Todd (1994). *Swim, Bike, Run.*

MOTIVATIONAL BOOKS:
Allen, Mark; Babbitt, Bob (1988). *Mark Allen's Total Triathlete.*
Armstrong, Lance (2000). *It's Not About The Bike, My Journey Back To Life.*
Armstrong, Lance (2003). *Every Second Counts.*
Parker, John L., Jr. (1978). *Once A Runner.*

ORGANIZATIONS:
*Challenged Athletes Foundation* (CAF)—www.challengedathletes.org
*Classic Race Management*—www.classicrace.com (race timing and results)
*GR Sports Center*—www.grsportscenter.com (sports medicine/rehab)
*Rapid Wheelmen*—www.lmb.org/rapidwheels/
*United States Cycling Association* (USCA)—www.usacycling.org
*United States Triathlon Association* (USAT)—www.usatriathlon.org

978-0-595-37703-9
0-595-37703-3

Printed in the United States
40446LVS00006B/400-450

9 780595 377039